Chambers Handbook for Judges' Law Clerks and Secretaries

Federal Judicial Center 1994

This Federal Judicial Center publication was undertaken in further-
ance of the Center's statutory mission to develop and conduct education programs for judicial branch employees. The views expressed are
those of the authors and not necessarily those of the Federal Judicial
Center.

Contents

Chapter 3. Basic Analysis of Litigation Conducted in U.S. Courts 23

Preface

In 1977, the Federal Judicial Center published the *Law Clerk Handbook*, co-authored by Judge Alvin B. Rubin and Anthony DiLeo, Esq. It was substantially revised in 1989 by Judge Rubin and Laura B. Bartell, Esq. In 1980, the Center published the *Handbook for Federal Judges' Secretaries*. Facing the need to update both publications, the Center, at the suggestion of a number of judicial branch employees, including secretaries, has combined these two handbooks into this *Chambers Handbook*. While the *Chambers Handbook* draws heavily from the *Law Clerk Handbook*, it should be valuable to judges' secretaries as well as law clerks.

The handbook provides an overview of chambers operations and the work of the federal courts; it does not provide detailed procedures on every aspect of a law clerk's or a secretary's daily tasks or review the procedures of each individual court (this is in large part because the duties of law clerks and judicial secretaries vary from court to court). Law clerks and secretaries should become familiar with local court procedures and inquire about a local chambers manual. More detailed information on personnel, administrative, and financial matters is in the *Guide to Judiciary Policies and Procedures,* published by the Administrative Office of the U.S. Courts.

Chapter 1. Introduction

§ 1-1. Function and Role of Law Clerks and Secretaries

The chambers staff assists with as many administrative and legal tasks as possible, leaving the judge more time for the nondelegable aspects of judging. Law clerks and secretaries have no statutorily defined duties; they carry out their judges' instructions. Because each judge decides cases in an individual manner and has developed work habits over the course of a professional career, no two judges use their staffs in precisely the same manner. Staff members must adjust to their judge's style and desires. Each member of the staff must work cooperatively with the other members so that, as a team, they effectively assist the judge in fulfilling his or her judicial responsibilities.

In most chambers, law clerks concentrate on legal research and writing, while secretaries have primary responsibility for administrative matters. Typically, law clerks' broad range of duties include the following: conducting legal research, preparing bench memos, drafting orders and opinions, editing and proofreading the judge's orders and opinions, and verifying citations. Many judges discuss pending cases with their law clerks and confer with them about decisions. Frequently, law clerks also maintain the library, assemble documents, serve as courtroom crier, handle exhibits during trial, and run errands for the judge. District court law clerks often attend conferences in chambers with attorneys.

Secretaries also help maintain the library, assemble documents, serve as courtroom crier, and run errands for the judge. In general, most secretaries assist in the day-to-day conduct of court business. In addition to traditional secretarial duties, a judge's secretary often deals with lawyers and members of the public on behalf of the judge. Since the secretary is generally the first member of a judge's staff whom outsiders meet, a pleasant, cheerful manner, together with a sincere effort to help visitors (and other staff), sets the tone for good working relationships. Secretaries must also be sensitive to the many demands made on judges and should help to shield them from unnecessary encroachments on their time. Specific aspects of this problem are discussed in several sections of this handbook.

Law clerks and secretaries for district court, bankruptcy court, and magistrate judges have substantially more contact with attorneys and witnesses than do their appellate court counterparts. The principal function of an appellate court law clerk is to research and write about the issues presented by an appeal, while law clerks for district, bankruptcy, and magistrate judges are involved in the many decisions made at every stage of each case. Chapter 5, "Chambers and Case Management," discusses in some detail the operations of district, bankruptcy, and appellate courts.

A clerkship can be viewed as a continuation of one's legal education. The education gained as a law clerk is practical; clerks participate in real court activity and decisions. They learn about law from the judge, who was formerly an accomplished practitioner or educator, and by attending trials, conferences, or oral arguments. The education is not limited to legal analysis: It includes exposure to the methods and customs of practitioners and the level of professional behavior expected of lawyers, as well as experience with the full range of legal styles and abilities presented in federal court. A clerkship provides direct insight into the judicial process, a unique opportunity for those interested in litigation or teaching. Moreover, law clerks face significant contemporary legal issues and have the opportunity to consider the social and economic implications of deciding cases that implicate those issues. Observing the challenging roles that judges and lawyers play in the resolution of controversies and contributing to that process add to the law clerk's professional development.

§ 1-2. History

For more than a century, chambers staff have aided federal judges in legal and administrative matters. Justice Horace Gray, appointed to the Supreme Court of the United States in 1881, introduced to that Court his practice (originally adopted while he was Chief Justice of the Supreme Judicial Court of Massachusetts) of employing, at his own expense, an honor graduate of Harvard Law School as his secretary. Gray's practice was continued by his successor on the Court, Justice Oliver Wendell Holmes.

In 1885, the Attorney General of the United States, in his report to Congress, recommended that each justice of the Supreme Court be "provided by law with a secretary or law clerk . . . to assist in such clerical work as might be assigned to him." In 1886, pursuant to that recommendation, Congress provided clerical assistants to the justices. In 1930, provision was made for law clerks for U.S. circuit court judges; in 1936, for U.S. district court judges; in 1979, for U.S. magistrate judges; and in 1984, for U.S. bankruptcy judges.

At present, each Supreme Court justice is authorized four law clerks (the Chief Justice is entitled to a fifth), and justices usually have a secretary and an assistant secretary. Each circuit judge is authorized a secretary, an assistant secretary, and up to three other persons as law clerks or assistant secretaries. Each district judge is authorized a law clerk, a secretary, and one additional person as a law clerk, assistant secretary, or court crier. Each bankruptcy judge is authorized one law clerk and one secretary. And each full-time magistrate judge is generally authorized one law clerk and one secretary. A chief district or chief circuit judge may employ an additional law clerk or secretary. In addition, all appellate and some district courts are authorized to employ staff attorneys, who serve the entire court.

§ 1-3. The Application Process

The first opportunity a prospective law clerk has to learn a particular judge's requirements is during the application process. Law schools often maintain helpful information about clerkship opportunities, including the appropriate time frame for submitting applications and what information should be sent to the judge. Some judges send clerkship applicants a written job description, which may include the duration of the appointment (usually one or two years), basic responsibilities, predominant types of litigation dealt with by the court, and other general information. A summary of this kind can help prospective applicants assess their interest, can shorten personal interviews, and can save the judge from repeating answers to questions commonly asked by applicants.

Prospective law clerks should take advantage of all opportunities to learn about the requirements of the specific job and the personal characteristics of the judge for whom they might work. Some judges encourage applicants whom they are seriously considering hiring to discuss frankly and confidentially with their incumbent staff the judge's personality, temperament, and work habits, so that the applicant can determine whether the relationship is likely to be rewarding. Judges—even those within the same district or city—are not fungible, and both judge and law clerk will likely find the employment experience more rewarding if they have a good match of interests and personality.

Whereas new law clerks are hired in most chambers each year, secretarial positions open sporadically. Although the application process for secretaries is generally less involved than for law clerks, it is important for prospective secretaries to obtain as much information as possible about the judge.

§ 1-4. Preparation and Reference Material

Law clerks and secretaries should acquire a paperbound copy of the Federal Rules of Criminal Procedure, the Federal Rules of Civil Procedure, and the Federal Rules of Evidence. In addition, law clerks and secretaries to bankruptcy judges will find a copy of the Bankruptcy Code and the Federal Rules of Bankruptcy Procedure indispensable, and law clerks and secretaries to appellate judges should have a copy of the Federal Rules of Appellate Procedure. Although the judge will have copies of these items in the library, a personal copy will help chambers staff become familiar with the rules. Law clerks and secretaries should also study carefully the local rules of court, standing orders, and other operating procedures.

The Federal Judicial Center has numerous publications dealing with federal court operations and with specific subjects such as summary judgment, copyright law, patent law, pretrial detention, employment discrimination, and bankruptcy law. Other Center publications, such as *Manual for Litigation Management and Cost and Delay Reduction* (1992), *Manual for Complex Litigation, Second* (2d ed. 1985), and *Bench Book for United States District Court Judges* (3d ed. 1986), contain specific information about case management and the judicial process in the trial court. "Introducing the Federal Courts," a Center video series that will have five parts when finished, introduces court employees to the operations of their particular courts. Law clerks and secretaries may wish to consult the Center's annual *Catalog of Publications* for a description of available written materials and the annual *Catalog of Audiovisual Media Programs* for audiocassettes and videotapes of possible interest.

Personal reference books will also be helpful. Each law clerk and secretary should have a dictionary, a thesaurus, a copy of *The Bluebook: A Uniform System of Citation (Fifteenth Edition)*, published by the Harvard Law Review Association, and the University of Chicago *Manual of Legal Citation*. It is also useful to have a stylebook, such as *The Chicago Manual of Style*, published by the University of Chicago Press; the *Harbrace College Handbook;* or the *Gregg Reference Manual*. Before writing the first assignment for a judge, every law clerk should read Strunk and White, *The Elements of Style* (3d ed.), and should periodically reread it.

A. Special Preparation for Law Clerks

After accepting an offer, the law clerk-to-be should inquire whether the judge recommends that his or her law clerks take any particular courses during their remaining time in law school. Every law clerk will benefit from courses in federal jurisdiction, federal civil procedure, evidence (including the Federal Rules of Evidence), criminal procedure, and constitutional law. In addition, a particular court may have a large volume of litigation in a particular area, and some judges may suggest that certain courses would be especially helpful. Law clerks should also consider background reading on the judicial process. Judge Ruggero J. Aldisert's *The Judicial Process* is a rich collection of readings and analysis. Judge Frank Coffin's *The Ways of a Judge* provides numerous insights into the decision-making process. Reading these works, as well as those cited immediately below, will help a prospective law clerk more fully understand both the judge's role and the law clerk's.

B. Suggested Supplementary Reading for Law Clerks

Bruce A. Ackerman, *In Memoriam: Henry J. Friendly*, 99 Harv. L. Rev. 1709 (1986)

Ruggero J. Aldisert, *Super Chief: Earl Warren and His Supreme Court*, 72 Ca. L. Rev. 275 (1984) (reviewing Bernard Schwartz, Super Chief: Earl Warren and His Supreme Court, a Judicial Biography (1983))

Paul R. Baier, *The Law Clerks: Profile of an Institution*, 26 Vand. L. Rev. 1125 (1973)

George D. Braden, *The Value of Law Clerks*, 24 Miss. L.J. 295 (1953)

Victor Brudney & Richard F. Wolfson, *Mr. Justice Rutledge—Law Clerk's Reflections*, 25 Ind. L.J. 455 (1950)

David Crump, *How Judges Use Their Law Clerks*, N.Y. St. B.J. 43 (May 1986)

Norman Dorsen, *Law Clerks in Appellate Courts in the United States*, 26 Mod. L. Rev. 265 (1963)

Arthur F. Fite III, *Law Clerkships—Three Inside Views*, 33 Ala. L. Rev. 155 (1972)

Nicholas Johnson, *What Do Law Clerks Do?*, 22 Tex. B.J. 229 (1959)

Judicial Clerkships: A Symposium on the Institution, 26 Vand. L. Rev. 1123 (1973)

Philip B. Kurland, *Jerome N. Frank, Some Reflections and Recollections of a Law Clerk*, 24 U. Chi. L. Rev. 661 (1957)

Earl D. Leach, *Recollections of a Holmes Secretary*, 1941 Harv. L. Sch. Bull. 12

Chief Judge T. John Lesinski, *Judicial Research Assistants: The Michigan Experience*, 10 Judges' J. 54 (1971)

Alfred McCormack, *A Law Clerk's Recollections*, 46 Colum. L. Rev. 710 (1946)

John B. Oakley & Robert S. Thompson, Law Clerks and the Judicial Process, Perceptions of the Qualities and Functions of Law Clerks in American Courts (1980)

C. Special Preparation for Secretaries

Secretaries should become familiar with the *Guide to Judiciary Policies and Procedures*, published by the Administrative Office of the U.S. Courts. The Administrative Office also distributes helpful directories, including the *United States Court Directory*, the *Directory of United States Probation and Pretrial Services Offices*, and the *Telephone Directory*. The *Telephone Directory* lists the telephone numbers and shows the organizational structure of the Administrative Office, the Federal Judicial Center, the Judicial Panel on Multidistrict Litigation, and the U.S. Sentencing Commission. For secretaries unfamiliar with the federal court system, *Federal Courts and What They Do*, a Federal Judicial Center publication, may be helpful.

§ 1-5. Orientation and Continuing Education

Many courts provide orientation programs for law clerks and secretaries, and some provide various kinds of local educational programs for court personnel generally or for the bar. Newly appointed law clerks and secretaries should ask whether the court has any such programs that are open to them. Typically, a personnel specialist in the office of the clerk of court can explain the government-wide and judiciary-wide policies and options.

New law clerks and secretaries should become familiar with the details of employee benefits (such as health insurance), policy regarding leave, and other particulars. On some matters, such as office hours and leave policy, the new employee should also learn the particular preferences of the judge. Some courts have other specific practices, such as awarding certificates of completion at the end of a law clerk's term.

Most court units have designated a training specialist who identifies local training needs and develops programs to meet those needs. District, bankruptcy, and appellate clerks' offices, probation and pretrial services offices, and circuit executives' offices usually have such a specialist. A secretary interested in obtaining more information on local training or continuing education should contact the clerk of court. The Federal Judicial Center provides technical assistance in the design and development of court training programs, including programs for judges' secretaries, and funding to supplement court funds.

Although the Federal Judicial Center provides continuing education and training for judges and permanent court employees, the

Board of the Center has determined, because of the temporary nature of law clerks' employment, that these Center resources cannot be made available to law clerks except in unusual circumstances. However, the Center has no objection to law clerks taking advantage of Center programs when this can be done at no cost to the Center. Law clerks may, for example, ask their judge or unit executive if it is appropriate for them to attend a local program. Also, as noted above, Center publications (such as this handbook) and audiovisual materials are available to judges' staffs.

Chapter 2. Conduct, Ethics, and Protocol

§ 2-1. Conduct and Ethics

Judicial branch employees must maintain exceptionally high standards of conduct. Not only judges, but their staffs, officials under judges' control, and all other employees of the judiciary should strive to maintain public confidence in the federal court system.

Law clerks and secretaries play important roles in the judicial process and must strive to maintain its integrity. Because of the close association among the judge and his or her personal staff, the professional and personal actions of law clerks and secretaries reflect on judges and ultimately on the judiciary as a whole. Law clerks and secretaries are therefore held to the very highest standards of conduct. Like judges, they hold a position of public trust and must comply with the demanding requisites of that position.

Though not comprehensive, the following survey of statutes, regulations, and resolutions of the Judicial Conference pertaining to the conduct of judicial employees and officials highlights areas of special concern.

While the Judicial Conference has adopted a code of conduct for law clerks, it has not yet adopted one for judges' secretaries.

A. Codes of Conduct

The Judicial Conference of the United States sets administrative policy for the federal courts. In 1973, the Conference adopted a resolution making the 1972 Code of Judicial Conduct of the American Bar Association (drafted originally for state judicial personnel) applicable to federal judges, with a few amendments and exceptions. In 1990, the Code was significantly revised. This Code is a successor to the ABA Canons of Judicial Ethics, first adopted in 1924.

B. Code of Conduct for Law Clerks

The Judicial Conference adopted the Code of Conduct for Law Clerks in March 1981 and has amended it several times since. The updated Code is reprinted in the Appendix to this handbook. The Code's seven canons should be followed in resolving ethical problems. Keep in mind, however, that the canons do not lessen more stringent standards established by law, court order, or the judge for whom the law clerk works. The Committee on the Codes of Conduct has published formal advisory opinions on issues frequently raised or issues of broad application. These opinions can be found in the *Guide to Judiciary Policies and Procedures*, Vol. II, Chapter IV. Further guidance in interpreting the Code may be sought from the Committee on the Codes of Conduct.

C. Committee on the Codes of Conduct

The Judicial Conference established a Committee on the Codes of Conduct: Persons covered by one of the codes of conduct adopted by the Conference may telephone or write the committee, through its chairperson, with questions about the applicability of the particular code to a contemplated action. Before contacting the committee, a law clerk should consult with the judge for whom the clerk works— the committee's guidance is only advisory and a final decision in any ethical situation is that of the staff member, in consultation with the judge.

The Committee on the Codes of Conduct should not be confused with another Conference committee, the Committee on Financial Disclosure, which was previously called the Judicial Ethics Committee. This committee receives financial disclosure reports (generally referred to by their form number, AO-10) from federal judges, magistrate judges, and judicial employees compensated in excess of the salary for Grade 16 of the General Schedule. Therefore, law clerks and secretaries are not required to complete this form.

D. Nepotism and Favoritism

The Code of Conduct for United States Judges, Canon 3B(4), states:

> A judge should not make unnecessary appointments and should exercise that power only on the basis of merit, avoiding nepotism and favoritism. A judge should not approve compensation of appointees beyond the fair value of services rendered.

Moreover, the Judicial Conference of the United States has resolved:

> No person should be appointed as law clerk or secretary to a circuit or district judge who is related to the judge concerned within the degree of [first cousin].

The U.S. Code also prohibits nepotism or favoritism in hiring and promoting law clerks and secretaries. *See* 5 U.S.C. § 3110(b), 28 U.S.C. § 458. Thus, a judge clearly may not hire a secretary or law clerk who is related to the judge as a first cousin or closer. In addition, many judges consider themselves prohibited from hiring the children or other relatives of close friends and from prevailing on other judges in the same court to do so. Though these rules may result in denial of a law clerkship or secretarial position to an otherwise qualified applicant, they prevent criticism of the court as an institution run for the personal benefit of a judge and the judge's family and friends. Inquiries regarding the propriety of hiring a particular individual may be referred to the General Counsel's Office of the Administrative Office.

E. Compensation for Extra-Judicial Activities; Honoraria

The Ethics Reform Act of 1989 prohibits a law clerk or secretary from personally receiving any honorarium during his or her tenure with the court. *See* 5 U.S.C. app. 7 § 501(b). "Honorarium" is "a payment of money or anything of value for an appearance, speech or article." 5 U.S.C. app. 7 § 505(3). The Judicial Conference has denoted the following *not* to be honorarium: compensation for approved teaching, compensation for any writing more extensive than an article, and a suitable, nonmonetary memento or token of no commercial value given in connection with an occasion or article. *See* Regulations of the Judicial Conference of the United States Under Title VI of the Ethics Reform Act of 1989 Concerning Outside Earned Income, Honoraria, and Outside Employment § 4, *in* Guide to Judiciary Policies and Procedures, Vol. II, Chapter V.

Although Canon 6 of the Code of Conduct for Law Clerks states, "A law clerk may receive compensation and reimbursement of expenses for all extra-official activities permitted by this Code" subject to certain restrictions, the stricter proscriptions of the Ethics Reform Act govern.

Because the Conference has delegated its administrative authority over Supreme Court employees under the Ethics Reform Act to the Chief Justice, before accepting honoraria, Supreme Court law clerks and secretaries should look to Court regulations for guidance.

F. Gifts

The Ethics Reform Act of 1989 proscribes the giving, solicitation, or acceptance of certain gifts by judicial branch officers and employees. *See* 5 U.S.C. §§ 7351, 7353. For example, a law clerk or secretary may not accept a gift in return for being influenced in the performance of any official act. 5 U.S.C. § 7353(b)(2)(B). Section C(2) of Canon 5 of the Code of Conduct for Law Clerks also restricts the types of gifts any law clerk may accept. The Judicial Conference has issued a set of regulations entitled *Regulations of the Judicial Conference of the United States Under Title III of the Ethics Reform Act of 1989 Concerning Gifts* to administer the Act.

Again, because the Conference has delegated its administrative authority over Supreme Court employees under the Ethics Reform Act to the Chief Justice, Supreme Court law clerks and secretaries should become familiar with regulations promulgated by the Chief Justice concerning gifts.

G. Political Activity

A September 1943 Judicial Conference resolution states that judicial branch employees should not participate in the kind of political activity forbidden to executive branch employees by the Hatch Political Activity Act as codified in Titles 5 and 18 of the U.S. Code. In general terms, the act prohibits federal government employees from actively participating in political campaigns in partisan elections. In 1993, Congress eased some of the Hatch Act restrictions, but, like the original act, these amendments do not apply officially to judicial branch employees.

Under the Hatch Act, government employees may express their views, wear candidates' buttons, contribute to campaigns, and belong to political parties, but may not make campaign speeches, solicit campaign contributions, or otherwise work on campaigns, organize political meetings, or serve as an officer of a political organization. These prohibitions do not apply to elections in which candidates do not run as representatives of the national political parties (such as many school board elections).

Canon 7 of the Code of Conduct for Law Clerks reads as follows:

> A law clerk should refrain from political activity; a law clerk should not act as a leader or hold office in a political organization; a law clerk should not make speeches for or publicly endorse a political organization or candidate; a law clerk should not solicit funds for or contribute to a political organization, candidate, or event; a law clerk should not become a candidate for political or public office; a law clerk should not otherwise engage in political activities.

Where the canon is stricter than the Act, the canon provides the applicable standard for law clerks. Thus, although the Act would permit it, law clerks may not wear campaign buttons or contribute funds to a political organization.

Law clerks and secretaries should never, even in private conversation, attribute to the judge any position on any legal or political issue. When asked about the judge's opinion on such a matter, law clerks and secretaries must indicate that they are not in a position to comment (unless the judge clearly does not object to such discussion). If judges wish to publicize their thoughts, they know how to do so.

H. Conflicts of Interest and Restrictions on the Practice of Law

Law clerks and secretaries may not ask for or receive compensation for "services rendered" in relation to any proceeding, determination, ruling, or matter in which the government has an interest. 18 U.S.C. § 203. Further, they must not act on behalf of individuals as attorneys or agents in matters affecting the government. 18 U.S.C. § 205. Section 205 prohibits, for example, a law clerk or secretary from acting as representative for an individual prosecuting a claim against the United States.

The Judicial Conference has resolved "[t]hat no person employed on a full-time basis in the federal judicial establishment shall engage in the private practice of law." Furthermore, section D of Canon 5 of the Code of Conduct for Law Clerks restricts law practice by law clerks.

The two rationales for applying this rule to law clerks are clear: First, practicing law could raise serious conflicts between a law clerk's obligations as a judicial employee, bound to impartiality, and his or her obligation to represent a client fully; and second, it would be nearly impossible for a law clerk to perform adequately and still have time for another job.

§ 2-2. Protocol

A. Confidentiality and Loyalty

Law clerks and secretaries owe the judge complete confidentiality. The judge relies on the law clerks' and secretaries' confidentiality in discussing performance of judicial duties, and must be able to count on their complete loyalty. Chambers staff must not criticize the judge's decisions or work habits to anyone, even other members of the same court. Unless expressly authorized by the judge, law clerks and secretaries should never comment on the judge's views or offer a personal appraisal of the judge's opinions; the judge is the only one who can or should communicate to the bar whatever personal views the judge wishes to have known publicly.

Judge Ruggero J. Aldisert describes the loyalty owed by a law clerk, and much of what he says is also applicable to secretaries:

> A judge's law clerk is a confidant. More than any other experience in preparing for a career in the legal profession, a clerkship is grounded on notions of confidentiality, pervasive in the practice of law. The judge–clerk relationship is as sacred as that of priest–penitent. Indeed, to emphasize the importance of this relationship, I give new law clerks a formal message:
>
> I have retained you as researchers and editors, but you are also my lawyers. As lawyers, you are absolutely forbidden to disclose the intimate details of this lawyer–client relationship, of the decision-making and decision-justifying processes that take place in these

chambers. This court is a family, and there will be times that I will make remarks about my family members. They will be uttered sometimes in the heat of passion or despair. They will not be repeated beyond the chambers door. Even if I occasionally blow off steam, remember that these judges are my colleagues and will be my friends long after you are gone from here.

Ruggero J. Aldisert, *Super Chief: Earl Warren and His Supreme Court*, 72 Ca. L. Rev. 275 (1984) (reviewing Bernard Schwartz, Super Chief: Earl Warren and His Supreme Court, a Judicial Biography (1983)).

B. Respect

Law clerks and judges have a special, multifaceted relationship: employee–employer, student–teacher, and lawyer–lawyer. In all of these roles, the law clerk must respect the judge. Respect does not mean subservience: A law clerk should not be afraid to express an opinion contrary to the judge's when asked; in fact, most judges expect and invite their law clerks to question the judges' views. Judges frequently seek the reactions of their law clerks to the issues raised in pending cases, both for the value of being exposed to varying viewpoints and to train their law clerks in the process of legal decision making. If, however, the judge should reach a conclusion that differs from the law clerk's, the law clerk should carry out the judge's instructions with the utmost fidelity. The ultimate responsibility for fulfilling the duties of the judge's office is the judge's. As one judge put it: "The commission from the President issues to me, not my law clerk, and it was I who took the oath of office."

C. Avoidance of Public Statement Regarding Pending or Past Proceedings

Law clerks' and secretaries' positions require discretion. Chambers staff must avoid any hint about the judge's likely action in a case. After the judge acts, the action (and, if there is an opinion, the reasoning underlying the action) is a matter of public record. Neither law clerks nor secretaries should comment on them or try to explain them. Further, chambers staff must scrupulously resist the temptation to discuss pending or decided cases among friends or family. Even discussions with law clerks and secretaries from other chambers should be circumspect. Indeed, some judges forbid their law clerks to discuss pending cases even with other law clerks.

Many district courts have rules forbidding court personnel to divulge information about pending cases. The duty to keep information confidential is grave; for example, willful violations of the Judicial Council of the District of Columbia's Confidentiality Rule may result in disciplinary action, dismissal, and prosecution for criminal contempt. If friends, representatives of news media, or others inquire concerning any proceeding, the law clerk or secretary may refer them to the official record in the office of the clerk of court.

D. Informing the Judge of Information Received Informally

The judge should be apprised of informal communications to law clerks and secretaries regarding pending cases. For example, an attorney may call to state that there is no objection to a pending motion, or that both attorneys jointly request the continuance of a hearing. Because of the impact of these events on docket management, the judge may wish to take some action. For example, the judge may wish to call a conference of counsel, or devote increased attention to another matter for which immediate preparation is necessary. Informal information can save the judge and the staff wasted effort.

A dilemma arises when the law clerk or secretary receives specific information about the progress of settlement negotiations in a case in which the judge is to be the trier of fact. Settlement proposals or discussions are ordinarily inadmissible at trial, and therefore some judges shield themselves from knowledge of settlement negotiations that might affect their judgment. Other judges either like to, or are willing to, have such information and are confident that they will not be influenced by it. Chambers staff must be guided by the policy of the individual judge in this regard.

E. Courtroom Demeanor

The law clerk, like the judge, is required to be impartial. During a jury trial, physical cues within view of the jurors may compromise impartiality and unfairly influence the jury. Even during a bench trial or appellate argument, law clerks must avoid movements or expressions that might indicate their reaction to testimony of witnesses or to oral arguments of attorneys, because impartiality and objectivity must always be maintained by everyone who is officially attached to the court. Indeed, litigants are more likely to expect and accept reflections of attitude by the judge, who has a duty to control proceedings and to decide the case, than by the judge's assistants.

F. Dress

Most judges do not have a formal dress code, but do expect the kind of professional dress and behavior that would be appropriate in a professional office.

G. The Public

The courts are a public-service organization, and the public properly expects efficient and professional service from them. The public generally is unfamiliar with the court system, and its opportunities to view the system in operation are infrequent. Every effort should be made to assist the public, including witnesses or jurors. The brief encounter that jurors or witnesses have with the federal court system may greatly influence their evaluation of the quality and efficiency of that system.

Courtesy and kindness, however, should not include advice. Absent permission from the judge, law clerks and secretaries must not answer questions about a case from witnesses or jurors.

H. The Media

1. Communication with the Media

Journalists frequently telephone chambers to inquire about a case, or attempt to provoke a conversation at a social affair. There should be as little communication as possible between chambers staff and representatives of the media. Law clerks and secretaries should ascertain the judge's policy with respect to the media and answer inquiries from members of the media accordingly. Some judges refer all questions to the clerk of court. Other judges direct the clerk of court to distribute opinions or judgments that are already in the public record.

2. Rules Regarding the Media in Court

Guidelines for allowing cameras and electronic reproduction equipment in the courtroom are published in the *Guide to Judiciary Policies and Procedures*, Vol. I, Chapter III, Part E. This policy was previously published as Canon 3A(7) in the Code of Conduct for U.S. Judges, but in September 1990, the Judicial Conference struck the canon and revised the policy, extending the permissible use of cameras and electronic reproduction equipment in the courtroom. Under the revised policy, a judge may authorize broadcasting, televising, recording, or taking photographs in the courtroom during ceremonial proceedings for any purpose. For nonceremonial proceedings, such activities in the courtroom may be allowed for presenting evidence, perpetuating a record of the proceedings, and for security or judicial administration purposes. (Canon 3A(7) limited nonceremonial use to "presentation of evidence" and "perpetuation of the record.") Except for courts participating in a pilot program (see below), the policy does not authorize contemporaneous broadcasting of nonceremonial proceedings from the courtroom to the public. The policy also does not authorize audiotaping or videotaping in the courtroom for subsequent dissemination to the public; the public has access to the official written record. Federal Rule of Criminal Procedure 53 prohibits photographing and radio broadcasting of criminal proceedings.

In 1990, the Judicial Conference authorized a three-year experiment permitting photographing, recording, and broadcasting of civil proceedings and appeals pursuant to special guidelines. The Federal Judicial Center is monitoring and evaluating the pilot. The participating courts are the Courts of Appeals for the Second and Ninth Circuits, the Southern District of Indiana, the District of Massachusetts, the Eastern District of Michigan, the Southern District of New York, the Eastern District of Pennsylvania, and the Western District of Washington.

In addition, the Judicial Conference gave the circuit judicial councils supervisory authority over the use of cameras in the courtroom in accordance with its guidelines, and some circuit councils have adopted specific instructions. Many district and appellate courts have local rules or standing orders regarding the relationship between the courts and the media. Law clerks and secretaries should review and be familiar with any local rule of the district or circuit relating to this topic and should assist in the enforcement of that rule.

Although local rules restrict the *means* by which news may be reported (e.g., no cameras or broadcasting from the courtroom or environs), "there is nothing that proscribes the press from reporting events that transpire in the courtroom." Sheppard v. Maxwell, 384 U.S. 333, 362–63 (1966). *See also* Nebraska Press Association v. Stuart, 427 U.S. 539 (1976). The Constitution creates a presumption that trials will be open. Press-Enterprise Co. v. Superior Court, 464 U.S. 501 (1984). This does not necessarily apply to pretrial proceedings (Waller v. Georgia, 467 U.S. 39 (1984)), but it does apply to argument of cases in both trial and appellate courts.

I. The Attorneys

Chambers staff should be friendly, courteous, and helpful to lawyers. At the same time, law clerks and secretaries should always keep in mind that they work for and are responsible to the judge, not to lawyers.

Law clerks and secretaries must be firm in resisting any effort by lawyers to gain improper advantage, to win favor, or to enlist sympathy. Nothing should be revealed to an attorney that could not be revealed to the general public. A few lawyers, perhaps because of their instincts as advocates, may attempt to gain information from chambers staff or to make a plea about the equity or justice of the result the lawyer is seeking. Law clerks and secretaries should not engage in any discussion with an attorney about a pending case or a decision that has been reached by the judge. Whatever the attorney has to say about a case should be set forth in a written pleading, memorandum, or letter, or by oral argument. Opposing counsel should receive copies of written materials or be present for oral argument. Ex parte communications create the atmosphere of partiality and potential unfairness and are of questionable value because the opposition may have a valid contrary argument that goes unheard.

Some judges forbid their law clerks to have any communication with lawyers. The law clerk for a judge who has this rule must respect it scrupulously. Other judges expect their law clerks to communicate or deal with lawyers in respect to some matters, such as scheduling. These judges want their law clerks to be helpful and cooperative, but nevertheless to avoid doing anything that will compromise the judge or the court staff. The law clerks for judges who have this policy should abide by the following precepts:

- The law clerk should not give any advice on matters of substantive law.

- If the lawyer asks about either local procedure or general federal procedure for handling a matter, the law clerk may read to the lawyer, or refer the lawyer to, the appropriate federal rule or local court rule. If the question relates to the judge's personal practice with respect to handling matters (e.g., requests for temporary restraining orders), the law clerk may tell the lawyer what the law clerk knows. The law clerk should not guess at what the judge does or may do. If not certain about the judge's policy, the law clerk should say something like, "I don't know what the judge would like a lawyer to do in these circumstances, but I'll be glad to consult the judge about the problem and call you back."

- The law clerk should not allow a lawyer to coax him or her into doing research, even the most minor.

- The law clerk should not hesitate to issue a disclaimer on any information he or she may give. Almost all attorneys understand such a position. ("I can't give you any legal advice, as you understand. However, you may find it helpful to look at local rule 3.09.")

- When in doubt, the law clerk should politely decline to give information. ("I'm really sorry I can't help you, but Judge X has instructed me not to answer that kind of question.")

Judges who want their law clerks to communicate with counsel about scheduling or other matters do not want the conversation to stray into anything that might reflect the judge's (or the law clerk's) attitude about the issues in the case. The sole authority on substantive or procedural issues is the judge, who communicates with the attorneys either verbally or through written opinions. Any expression by the law clerk to an attorney about a pending case may raise the expectations or dash the hopes of the lawyer, or influence the lawyer's strategy in further proceedings—without authority or propriety. Such expressions impute exaggerated importance to the law clerk and destroy faith in the deliberative nature of the judicial process.

1. Neutrality and Impartiality

All attorneys should be given impartial and equal treatment. Law clerks and secretaries should resist the temptation to do a favor for a former classmate or an old friend.

Problems may arise if a law clerk is applying for a position with a lawyer or law firm then appearing in pending cases. This problem is discussed in section 2-2.J.1 *infra*.

2. Prior Notice to Counsel

Generally, if an attorney asks when an opinion will be rendered, the law clerk or secretary should indicate that such information is confidential, unless the judge has instructed otherwise. In cases of interest to the general public or media, however, some judges may wish to notify the attorneys in advance when a prospective judgment, opinion, or order is to be filed (except when such information might provide the attorneys and parties with "inside" information of potentially significant economic advantage). Such notice enables counsel to read the opinion at the moment it is filed and notify their clients of the result. Attorneys appreciate the opportunity to be the first to notify their clients, and clients themselves may wish to notify other interested parties of the result. Some embarrassment and confusion may result if the parties first hear of a ruling through the media. Moreover, media reports are often incomplete and misleading.

J. Restrictions on Law Clerks

1. Involvement in Cases of Attorneys with Whom Applications for Employment Are Pending

Application by a law clerk to a firm that has cases pending before the judge may create problems for the law firm, the judge, and the law clerk. Practices regarding this matter vary. Some judges instruct their law clerks not to apply for jobs with law firms until near the end of the clerkship. Others permit applications, but exclude the law clerk from all matters in which that firm is involved, requiring another law clerk to handle such matters. The law clerk should learn the judge's policy and follow it. In any event, even if no restrictions are placed on a law clerk's applications for employment, a commonsense rule is that a law clerk should carefully avoid even the most indirect discussion of cases pending before the judge during interviews and other communications with the firm. When law clerks accept a position with an attorney or firm, they should cease further involvement in those cases in which the future employer has an interest.

2. Practice After Termination of a Clerkship: Cases in Which the Law Clerk Was Involved; Appearances Before the Judge for Whom the Law Clerk Worked

Many courts or individual judges place restrictions on a law clerk's professional activities after the end of the clerkship. These may include prohibitions from ever participating in any form in any case pending during the law clerkship, or prohibitions from appearing as an attorney in the court in which the law clerk served, usually for one or two years. The law clerk must determine the policy of both the court and the judge. In any event, former law clerks must not participate in a case in which they performed work of any kind while law clerks. The ABA's Model Rules of Professional Responsibility also prohibit lawyers from representing a client in a case on which the lawyer worked previously as a public officer or employee. Some courts have adopted rules relating to these matters, and the law clerk is, of course, bound to follow these rules.

Chapter 3. Basic Analysis of Litigation Conducted in U.S. Courts

Litigation in the federal courts is governed by a number of nationally applicable rules: the Federal Rules of Civil Procedure, the Federal Rules of Criminal Procedure, the Federal Rules of Appellate Procedure, the Federal Rules of Bankruptcy Procedure, and the Federal Rules of Evidence. These are supplemented by the local rules of each individual court and standing orders of individual judges. Law clerks and secretaries should keep a copy of these uniform and local rules at hand.

The following section outlines the process of civil litigation.

§ 3-1. The Civil Action

A. Federal Jurisdiction

Federal courts are courts of limited jurisdiction; they may hear only those cases described in Article III, section 2 of the Constitution and authorized by Congress. Most civil cases in federal court are based on either of two types of jurisdiction: "federal question" jurisdiction (28 U.S.C. § 1331) or "diversity of citizenship" jurisdiction (28 U.S.C. § 1332). Federal question jurisdiction applies to cases involving the Constitution, federal laws, or treaties of the United States. Under diversity of citizenship jurisdiction, a claim based on state law may be brought in federal court if it exceeds $50,000 and plaintiffs and defendants are from different states. In addition, federal courts have jurisdiction over other special areas, such as bankruptcy cases, trademark and copyright violations, and incidents at sea. *See* 28 U.S.C. §§ 1331–1367.

B. Processing Litigation

The major steps in civil cases are as follows:

- Plaintiff commences action by filing a complaint with the clerk of court.

- Personal jurisdiction is obtained over defendant (e.g., by service of process).

- Defendant files motions (e.g., motion to dismiss for failure to state a claim for which relief may be granted—certain motions must be filed in defendant's first responsive pleading, while others may be filed later).

- Defendant files an answer, which may contain a motion to dismiss.

- Discovery proceeds.

- Either party may file additional motions (e.g., summary judgment).

- Pretrial conference is held.

- Trial is held.

- Judgment is rendered, signed, and filed.

- Post-trial proceedings may occur.

- Appeal may be taken—judgment may or may not be stayed.

- Appeal is considered either on briefs or after oral argument.

- Judgment is rendered on appeal.

- Supplementary proceedings may occur.

- Judgment is enforced.

In any given case, some of these steps may be omitted because of inaction, agreement of the parties, or court order. And, of course, the suit may end by settlement or dismissal at any stage. Fewer than 10% of all civil actions continue to trial, but the court decides motions in many cases that don't make it to trial.

C. Commencement of Action

A civil action in a federal court begins with the filing of a written complaint in the clerk's office. The case is then assigned a number, usually referred to as a "docket number," containing two parts: the last two digits of the year in which the case was filed, and a number that is assigned consecutively as suits are filed in each calendar year, usually beginning with number 101 (but in some courts beginning with the number 1). The prefix "Cr." or "C.A." indicates whether the case is a criminal or civil action. Thus, the thirty-seventh civil case filed in 1988 would be assigned the number C.A. 88-137. (In those courts where suits begin with the number 1, the case number would be C.A. 88-37.) In a multijudge court, the clerk's office, through a preestablished random selection process, immediately assigns the case to a particular judge for handling and ultimate disposition. The clerk then adds a section designation, usually a letter, to the docket number to indicate the section of the district court to which the case has been assigned or to indicate in which division of the court the case was filed.

The clerk's office maintains the complete record of the case, a case file, or docket sheet (which includes notations to reflect the progress of the case), and alphabetical indices by parties' names (which allow retrieval of the number of a case). Each month the clerk's office submits a statistical report to the Administrative Office describing each case that has been filed (Form JS-5).

In most cases there is little to be done in the judge's chambers when the case is filed except to make such record entries as may be used by the judge to monitor and control the progress of the case. If, however, there is a request for a temporary restraining order or other immediate emergency relief, or if the case is a class action, early attention is required. Some judges briefly review (or have their clerks review) all newly filed complaints to identify those that appear frivolous, lack federal jurisdiction, or are otherwise susceptible to fast-track handling.

The local rules of court usually require the lawyer who files a class action to indicate its nature by a caption on the first page of the complaint. Federal Rule of Civil Procedure 23(c)(1) requires: "As soon as practicable after the commencement of an action brought as a class action, the court shall determine by order whether it is to be so maintained." The judge will usually wish, therefore, to be promptly alerted to the filing of class actions. Other proceedings requiring prompt action by the court are discussed below.

D. Multidistrict Litigation Problems

If civil actions involving one or more common questions of fact are pending in different districts, either the plaintiff or defendant may petition the Judicial Panel on Multidistrict Litigation (JPMDL) to transfer the cases to a single district and to consolidate them for pretrial proceedings. *See* 28 U.S.C. § 1407. The rules of the panel are found in the rules section of Title 28 and in the *Manual for Complex Litigation*, available in the judge's library. If the panel decides that the cases should be consolidated, it enters an appropriate order and all of the cases are transferred to the district designated by the panel.

The district judge may independently invoke intervention of the JPMDL by writing the panel at the address listed in the *United States Court Directory*. The letter should say that the court has a case that may be related to a case or cases pending in another district, giving the name and docket number of each case, and that it might be worthwhile for the panel to examine these cases to determine whether pretrial consolidation would be appropriate. The judge will attach to the letter a copy of the complaint in the case pending in his or her court and any other documents that may be useful to the panel. The judge might also wish to send copies to counsel.

The functions of the JPMDL are discussed at section 3-5.D.1 *infra*. Any unanswered questions about multidistrict litigation procedures should be directed to the law clerk of the panel, who is listed in the *United States Court Directory*.

E. Service of Summons and Complaint; Waiver of Service

The Federal Rules of Civil Procedure give the plaintiff the option of notifying a defendant of the commencement of a lawsuit by (1) serving the defendant with a summons and a copy of the complaint, or (2) providing the defendant with written notice of the lawsuit, along with a request that the defendant waive service of the summons, in order to avoid the costs of service. Service of a summons or filing a waiver of service establishes jurisdiction over the person of a defendant, subject to the territorial limits upon effective service contained in Federal Rule of Civil Procedure 4(k).

A plaintiff electing to serve a summons on a defendant may present the summons to the deputy clerk either upon or after filing the complaint. If the summons is in proper form, the clerk signs it, places the seal of the court on it, and issues it to the plaintiff for service on the defendant. A summons (or a copy of the summons, if it is addressed to multiple defendants) must be issued for each defendant to be served.

If the summons and complaint are not served upon a defendant within 120 days after filing of the complaint, the court may dismiss the action without prejudice as to that defendant, or direct that service be effected within a specified time if the plaintiff shows good cause for the failure to serve within the 120-day limit. The court may take this action upon motion or upon its own initiative, after notice to the plaintiff.

Service may be made by any person eighteen years of age or older who is not a party. At the request of the plaintiff, the court may direct that service be made by a U.S. marshal or by another person or officer specially appointed by the court. Service must be made by a marshal or other specially appointed person when the plaintiff is authorized to proceed

- in forma pauperis, pursuant to 28 U.S.C. § 1915; or

- as a seaman, under 28 U.S.C. § 1916.

If service is not waived or made by a person specially appointed by the court, the person making service is required to furnish proof of service to the court in the form of an affidavit. Fed. R. Civ. P. 4(l).

If a plaintiff elects to request a defendant to waive service, and provides the defendant with proper notice of the request and lawsuit pursuant to the provisions of Federal Rule of Civil Procedure 4(d)(2), the defendant has a duty to avoid the unnecessary costs involved in serving the summons.

If a defendant located within the United States fails to comply with a request for waiver made by a plaintiff located in the United States, the court will impose the costs subsequently incurred by the plaintiff in effecting service on the defendant, unless the defendant shows good cause for the failure to waive. A defendant making timely return of a waiver avoids those costs, and is not required to serve an answer to the complaint until sixty days after the date on which the request for waiver was sent (ninety days if the defendant was addressed outside a judicial district of the United States). A defendant is allowed to return the waiver within thirty days of the date on which the request was sent (sixty days from that date if the defendant is addressed outside any judicial district of the United States).

The waiver of service provisions of Rule 4 apply to individuals, corporations, or associations otherwise subject to service under the rule. They do not apply to infants, incompetent persons, the United States, or agencies, corporations, or officers of the United States. These defendants must be served with copies of the summons and complaint in the manner made applicable to them by Rule 4.

Rule 4 also contains provisions regulating the manner in which service may be effected upon individuals located in the United States, individuals located in a foreign country, corporations and associations, the United States (including its agencies, corporations, or officers), state and local governments, and foreign states.

F. Motion Practice

After the complaint is filed, the defendant may respond with motions, an answer, or both. Law clerks may be asked to perform any or all of the following duties in connection with a motion:

- Maintain in-office records and call to the judge's attention motions that are ready for decision;

- Read and analyze the motion, any responses, and briefs;

- Perform independent research supplementary to that contained in the briefs of the parties;

- Attend hearings;

- Prepare memoranda for use by the judge regarding factual or legal issues presented by the motion;

- Discuss the motion with the judge; and

- Draft, for the judge's approval, an order disposing of the motion.

Secretaries may be asked to maintain the in-office records and help prepare the orders.

The motions most frequently filed early in proceedings are those challenging jurisdiction of the court over the parties or the subject matter, attacking venue, raising issues relating to joinder of parties, and denying the legal sufficiency of the complaint. Some courts refuse to accept a motion for filing with the clerk of court unless a memorandum of law is filed simultaneously. Although some courts do not require reply memoranda, opposing counsel are usually required to file a memorandum of law if the motion is opposed.

Upon receipt of a motion or a response to a motion, the clerk of court makes appropriate record entries and then routes the motion and supporting papers to the judge assigned to the case. Many courts require all motions, responses to motions, and supporting memoranda to be filed in duplicate so that one copy may be retained in the record and the other used in the judge's chambers. The judge's office usually maintains a list of all pending motions.

Some motions are perfunctory and can be ruled on without a hearing or oral argument. The law clerk must know the judge's preference in this regard, as some judges hear oral argument on all motions. Other judges require moving counsel to request oral argument in the body of the motion, state the reason why counsel believes oral argument would be helpful to the court, and provide an estimate of the time required for the argument. The court may then, in its discretion, set the motion for argument and notify counsel in writing of the day and time. Still other courts hear argument unless the judge notifies counsel that the matter will be decided on the briefs.

The local rules of the district court usually require a party opposing a motion to respond within a certain number of days after the motion is filed or at least a certain number of days before the date set for hearing.

Some motions involve disputed factual issues and therefore require evidentiary hearings. These and all motions for which the judge has requested oral argument must be scheduled at times convenient for the court and, insofar as possible, for counsel and witnesses. Four different approaches to scheduling have been adopted:

- Selection of a specific date and time by the judge or judge's staff with notice to both counsel;

- Selection of a date and time convenient for all involved after telephone or personal conferences among counsel and court personnel;

- Selection of a date and time acceptable to the court by one attorney who then gives notice to other counsel; and

- Permanent scheduling by the court of a weekly or monthly "motion day" at which any motions that are at issue may be heard as a matter of course, or, alternatively, for which particular motions are scheduled through one of the processes described above.

In some courts in which a number of motions are heard on a single day, the following procedure is used. Several days in advance, the docket clerk or courtroom deputy prepares a list of the motions to be heard on a particular day, including the names of the cases and docket numbers. For each motion, a law clerk or secretary assembles the record, a copy of each memorandum, and all other relevant materials. (In addition, for motions of any complexity, some judges ask a law clerk to draft a bench memo summarizing the issues. Judges usually do some preparation in advance of the hearing date.) These are brought to the courtroom a short time before the opening of court and are placed close to the judge's bench. A large number of motions may be scheduled, and the assembly of records and materials may be time-consuming. Organization and preparation are the keys to efficiency. Attorneys in a case are responsible for ensuring that witnesses are present at evidentiary hearings—either voluntarily or through use of subpoena. To avoid protracted waiting periods for other lawyers who have motions to be heard on the same day, most courts that have a regular "motion day" do not permit testimony to be heard on that day without a special order from the judge.

In courts that hear oral argument on a number of motions on the same day, it is not unusual for the court to receive requests for a continuance of the argument on motions. The date may have been set originally by one lawyer without finding out whether opposing counsel had a prior commitment; lawyers may have appearances scheduled before more than one judge on the same day; opposing counsel may request more time to study the law and facts and to prepare a memorandum opposing the motion; or the lawyers may believe they can resolve the issue between themselves. For any of these reasons, one or both lawyers may request a continuance.

Many judges will agree to continue a motion based on a lawyer's telephone request if the lawyer advises the judge that opposing counsel has been informed of the request and has no objection. Other judges require counsel to file a written motion for a continuance, even when opposing counsel has no objection. The motion or an attached memorandum must state the reason for the proposed continuance and fix a day on which the motion will be heard.

A law clerk usually assists the judge during the motions-day arguments by making available any materials relevant to a particular motion, by noting any new authority cited by either counsel, and, if the judge decides the motion from the bench, by making notes of the judge's decision (though the courtroom deputy officially records the court's judgment or decision and the judge later signs a summary order prepared by that deputy or submitted by prevailing counsel). When all responses and briefs have been filed or the allowed time has elapsed and, in appropriate cases, oral argument or an evidentiary hearing has been held, the motion is ripe for decision. (The term frequently used is that the motion is "at issue.")

Helping to ensure that the judge is prepared whenever he or she takes the bench is among a law clerk's most important duties. Accordingly, clerks must keep abreast of the motion calendar and be familiar with time limits under local rules.

G. Opinions on Motions Under Submission

Whenever the judge hears argument on a motion and does not rule from the bench, it is necessary to prepare an order disposing of the motion. If the judge instructs a law clerk to do this, the clerk should start by asking the judge's secretary for samples of orders previously issued that can serve as guides. The judge may instead direct one of the parties to prepare the order for court approval. *See infra* section 7-2.F.6.

After an order ruling on the motion has been signed, it is sent to the office of the clerk of court, where appropriate record entries are made. The clerk's office then notifies all attorneys of record of the ruling by the court and usually sends them a photocopy of the order.

Matters taken under submission must be carefully followed to be sure they are decided as promptly as possible. The secretary or law clerk should keep a list of matters under submission, deleting cases as the ruling on each is completed.

H. Temporary Restraining Orders

The procedural rules governing applications for temporary restraining orders are set forth in Federal Rule of Civil Procedure 65. When such orders are sought, plaintiff's counsel may assert that the matter is of such urgency as to require an ex parte restraining order, that is, without prior notice to or opportunity to be heard by the defendant. If the judge is not in chambers at the time, the plaintiff's counsel may exhort the law clerk or secretary to bring the order to the judge in open court, or to locate the judge, or to assist in some other way. The chambers staff should inquire about the judge's policy on such emergency inquiries so as to be prepared to handle them.

Most district judges will not sign requests for ex parte temporary restraining orders except in dire emergencies where the exigencies of the situation do not permit the opposing party to be heard, and then only after full compliance with Rule 65(b). If a lawyer comes to the chambers asking to see the judge about signing an ex parte temporary restraining order, some judges may wish their chambers staff to do the following:

- Advise the lawyer that the judge does not ordinarily sign temporary restraining orders without hearing what the lawyer for the other side has to say. This may be done by arranging for the judge to see both counsel in person or by a telephone conference, depending on the judge's policy. The staff should communicate with the judge to determine when the conference should be scheduled.

- While the lawyer is attempting to arrange the conference, law clerks should attempt to read all documents pertinent to the request, collect and examine the authorities, and be prepared to brief the judge about the request or to take such other action as the judge may wish.

- Communicate with the courtroom deputy and the court reporter to arrange for their presence at the conference if the judge requires their presence.

- In the absence of the judge, the clerk may be authorized to discuss with counsel whether they can agree to maintain the status quo until the judge is available.

I. The Answer

Twenty days after the complaint is served, or ten days after notice of disposition of a preliminary motion, the defendant must answer the complaint. If the defendant fails to do so, the plaintiff may have the defendant's default made a matter of record in the clerk's office and then proceed to obtain a default judgment in the manner provided in Federal Rule of Civil Procedure 55.

In addition to answering the complaint, the defendant may assert a counterclaim against a plaintiff or a cross claim against another defendant. The party against whom a counterclaim or cross claim is made has twenty days after service or ten days after disposition of a motion relating to the counterclaim or cross claim in which to reply. In the event of a failure to answer, the defendant may obtain a default judgment in accordance with Rule 55.

Many courts permit counsel, by agreement, to extend the time for answering. Other courts believe that an appearance of some kind— even if only to obtain an extension of time—should be made by counsel so that the court can be promptly informed of counsel's identity and will have the means to determine what progress is being made. To this end, some courts have adopted a rule that provides the following:

> Upon certification by a moving party that there has been no previous extension of time to plead and that the opposing party has not filed in the record an objection to an extension of time, then on an ex parte motion and order, the court will allow one extension for a period of 20 days from the time the pleading would otherwise be due. Further extensions will not be granted by stipulation but only after motion noticed for hearing according to the regular motion procedure.

Motions relating to third-party practice or to jurisdiction over or sufficiency of a counterclaim or cross claim may be filed at this stage of the proceedings. They are processed in the same manner as preliminary motions.

J. Alternative Dispute Resolution

Courts have developed several forms of court-annexed Alternative Dispute Resolution (ADR) over the past decade, primarily to promote settlement. (Litigants may, of course, agree to avail themselves of private ADR programs that are not affiliated with the court.) The Civil Justice Reform Act of 1990, which directs all courts to consider the adoption of an ADR program (28 U.S.C. § 473(a)(6)), has led to increased use of these programs. Both this act and other statutes have established ADR pilot programs in courts.

Some ADR programs may be more suitable for certain types of cases than others. Following is a brief description of the principal court-annexed programs.

Law clerks and secretaries should inquire which (if any) ADR programs are used in their courts, exactly what involvement their judges tend to have with such programs, and what assistance is expected.

1. Arbitration

The litigants present their cases to an outside neutral (or panel of neutrals) called an arbitrator (or arbitrators). Attorneys from the local community generally serve as the arbitrators. The presentations are generally less formal than a trial, and the rules of evidence are suspended. The arbitrator issues a nonbinding decision. If the parties accept the decision, the case is terminated with no right to appeal. If the parties do not accept the decision, they may proceed to trial or may agree on an outcome different from the arbitrator's decision. Arbitration promotes settlement, even when parties reject the arbitrator's decision, by suggesting the likely outcome should the parties proceed in court.

Currently twenty courts are authorized to have court-annexed arbitration programs. Ten are designated as mandatory arbitration courts, in which certain classes of cases (generally those involving money damages under $100,000) automatically go to arbitration unless a party files and the court grants a motion for exemption. *See* Barbara Meierhoefer, Court-Annexed Arbitration in Ten District Courts (Federal Judicial Center 1990). Ten other courts are authorized to have voluntary arbitration, in which parties use arbitration if they choose to. The statute authorizing the twenty arbitration courts (28 U.S.C. §§ 651–658) expires December 31, 1994, and it is not clear at this time what action Congress will take.

2. Mediation

The litigants meet with an outside neutral, either court-appointed or selected by the litigants, for in-depth settlement discussions. Mediators, who are sometimes but not always experts in the subject matter of the case and who are usually attorneys, do not render a decision. They assist the litigants in identifying key issues and developing a settlement package. If the case does not settle, the parties may proceed to trial.

3. Early Neutral Evaluation (ENE)

Early in the case, the court refers the litigants to an outside neutral, who is an attorney with expertise in the subject matter of the case. The parties each present their side to the early neutral evaluator, who then offers an opinion about the case's likely outcome. Settlement is facilitated by enhancing communication and providing litigants with a more realistic assessment of their prospects. Even if settlement does not occur, the issues for trial may be narrowed and the cost and duration of litigation reduced.

4. Nonbinding Summary Jury Trial

The court conducts an abbreviated trial before a regularly impaneled jury. The jury offers a nonbinding verdict, and the lawyers are generally permitted to question the jurors about their decision. Settlement is promoted by giving the parties an idea of the likely outcome if they go to trial. If the case does not settle, the parties may proceed to trial.

5. Nonbinding Summary Bench Trial

The same as a summary jury trial, except tried to the judge.

6. Settlement Weeks

The court designates a specific time period, generally one or two weeks once or twice a year, during which parties in many cases are referred to neutral attorneys for settlement discussions. The settlement discussions are held at the court house.

K. The Dormant Action

Most federal courts do not permit actions to remain dormant for an indefinite period of time. Each court, and sometimes the judges within each court, will have a different policy with respect to this. Counsel have their own priorities for processing litigation, and these frequently relate to their internal office demands and other personal matters. In general, however, the policy of the federal courts is that litigation is not merely the lawyers' business but also the public's business, and the court is responsible for monitoring it.

To fulfill this responsibility, many courts have the docket clerk or someone in the clerk of court's office periodically call to the judge's attention cases that have been dormant for more than six months (or some other period of time) because either no answer was filed or, after pleadings were filed, no further action was taken. Many judges will have a periodic "docket call," at which counsel will be asked to report on the status of cases that have been dormant for a certain period of time and to explain the lack of progress. In some instances, failure of counsel to appear at the docket call results in dismissal of the case.

The Civil Justice Reform Act of 1990 (28 U.S.C. §§ 471–482) mandated that each district court implement a plan for civil justice delay and expense reduction. Chambers staff in district courts should be familiar with whatever plan is in effect in their district, as it may impose deadlines or rules that affect case management. Chambers staff should also inquire about the plan's relationship to the court's local rules, which also contain deadlines and other requirements that affect case management.

L. Motion Practice After Answer

1. Discovery Motions and Schedules

The purpose of discovery is to allow each party to obtain relevant evidence or sources of relevant evidence from other parties and to avoid evidentiary surprise at the time of trial. General provisions governing discovery are set forth in Federal Rule of Civil Procedure 26. The specific discovery methods available to a party are as follows:

- Deposition on oral examination (Rule 30);

- Deposition on written questions (Rule 31);

- Interrogatories to parties (Rule 33);

- Production of documents and things (Rule 34);

- Permission to enter upon land and other property for inspection and other purposes (Rule 34);

- Physical and mental examinations (Rule 35); and

- Requests for admission of fact (Rule 36).

In routine cases, counsel conduct discovery proceedings without direct initial court involvement. Federal Rule of Civil Procedure 16, however, directs judges to intervene early in the suit to assume judicial control over its progress and to schedule dates for completion of the principal pretrial steps, including discovery. The rule mandates a pretrial scheduling order except in categories of actions exempted by local rule. In complex cases, in cases assigned by the Judicial Panel on Multidistrict Litigation, and in cases in which the court is attempting to reduce the time spent on discovery, the court also becomes directly involved by scheduling times and places for discovery activities and otherwise monitoring and supervising such proceedings.

A variety of motions may arise as a result of discovery proceedings, including those

- to compel answers or other compliance with discovery rules;

- to obtain protective orders against undue harassment, unreasonable demands, or disclosure of confidential or protected information;

- to obtain additional time to comply with discovery requests;

- to terminate a deposition;

- to pose objections to written interrogatories or other discovery requests; and

- to impose sanctions for failure to comply with discovery requests.

Federal Rule of Civil Procedure 26 prescribes general rules governing discovery. Amendments to Rule 26 that went into effect on December 1, 1993, require parties to disclose to each other certain types of information without waiting for a formal discovery request. These disclosures must be exchanged prior to the initial Rule 16 conference. The amended rule also requires parties to confer prior to the initial Rule 16 conference to develop a discovery plan, which they must submit to the court prior to the conference. Amended Rule 26 permits each district court and individual judge to decide whether to apply certain of its disclosure requirements to cases filed in that court or before that judge. Many of the discovery rules amended in 1993 allow exceptions to be made by local rule, agreement of the parties, or court order. Chambers staff should discuss with their judge which rules apply in their court.

In many courts, all motions pertaining to discovery are referred to a magistrate judge, as is responsibility for overseeing discovery procedures and ruling on discovery motions. The magistrate judge's orders may be appealed to the district judge.

2. Summary Judgment and Amended Pleadings Motions

During discovery or after its completion, other motions may be filed. These tend to fall into two categories:

- Motions for summary judgment as to some or all of the issues raised in the case (Rule 56); and

- Motions to amend pleadings or to add or remove parties (Rule 15).

Both usually arise out of information obtained by the moving party during discovery. They are processed in the same manner as other motions.

M. Pretrial Conference

The pretrial conference is governed by Federal Rule of Civil Procedure 16 and is intended to simplify the subsequent trial. Whether to hold a conference in a specific case is discretionary with the court, and the practice varies substantially throughout the federal judiciary. In many courts a pretrial conference is routinely held in each case, while in a few courts a conference is held only when requested by counsel or ordered by the court. Other courts ordinarily hold a pretrial conference, but exempt routine cases such as government collection and Social Security.

Some judges prefer not to hold the conference until some discovery has taken place, so that counsel are more aware of the evidence in the case. Increasingly, however, judges are holding pretrial conferences early in the proceedings to establish discovery schedules and other preliminary matters. Additional conferences may be conducted as the case progresses.

Prior to the pretrial conference, the law clerk or secretary should review the case file, put the documents in sequence, and place both the file and the record in the judge's chambers in the place designated by the judge. This should be done sufficiently in advance of the conference to allow the judge time to look through the file. A proposed pretrial order that has been submitted should be placed at the top of the file.

Some judges may want the courtroom deputy, the law clerk, or both to attend pretrial conferences. Others permit their law clerks to attend selected conferences of interest. During the first month or two after beginning work, the law clerk should attend as often as possible to gain insight into the conference procedure.

During the conference, the judge and counsel may consider any "matters that may aid in the disposition of the action." The matters most commonly considered are

- Simplification of the issues;
- Necessary or desirable amendments to the pleadings;
- The avoidance of unnecessary evidence at trial by obtaining admissions of uncontested facts;
- Limitation of the number of expert witnesses;
- Referral of issues to a special master;
- Exchange of lists of witnesses;
- Marking of exhibits;
- Final discovery procedures; and
- Settlement.

In many courts, counsel are required to file and exchange detailed pretrial memoranda containing information relating to the matters to be considered at the conference. Issues that can be effectively addressed at the pretrial conferences are described in the Federal Judicial Center's *Manual for Litigation Management and Cost and Delay Reduction* (1992) at pp. 5–21.

The conference itself may be held in chambers, with or without a court reporter, or may be conducted as a formal hearing in open court.

Some courts have adopted a local rule describing the pretrial procedure. In other courts, judges issue photocopied descriptions of their pretrial procedure. The law clerk should inquire about the judge's practice, study any applicable court rule or standing order, and be prepared to assist in any way possible.

N. Pretrial Orders

In civil cases other than those involving simple issues of law or fact, Federal Rule of Civil Procedure 16 requires a scheduling order (within 120 days of filing) and specifies matters to be discussed at any pretrial conference held pursuant to the rule, followed by a pretrial order. Almost all district courts have adopted a form for the pretrial order. Usually the court requires the pretrial order to contain a concise summary of disputed issues of fact and law, a succinct statement of the position of each party, and a list of the witnesses and documents expected to be introduced at trial. In some districts, the final pretrial order must be presented to the court at least twenty-four hours before the face-to-face pretrial conference, which is held with all lawyers and the judge present. Other courts require only that counsel bring the pretrial order with them to the conference.

Preparation of a detailed pretrial order often requires a substantial amount of time. Judges differ on whether the results warrant the effort. Those judges who require such an order usually demand that the opposing attorneys meet face-to-face to prepare it, for its preparation requires counsel to be familiar with the case from both their point of view and that of their opponents. Most judges consider a properly prepared pretrial order essential to an orderly and efficient trial of a complicated case. In simpler cases, judges may require counsel to prepare only a list of witnesses and exhibits.

Once the pretrial order is signed by the judge and the lawyers at the pretrial conference, most judges will not allow amendments to include new witnesses or documents unless special justification is shown for their not having been included originally.

An individual judge may want the lawyers to incorporate something other than what the local rules require. For this reason the law clerk should learn not only what the local rules of court require with respect to pretrial orders and conferences, but also the practice of the judge.

O. Sanctions

At least since the 1970s, many judges and lawyers have been concerned about abuse of the litigation process—for example, attorneys who file needless motions or are unprepared for trial or pretrial events. In 1983, the Judicial Conference proposed, and Congress accepted, amendments to the Federal Rules of Civil Procedure to assist the judges in dealing with this perceived problem. These amendments—to Rules 7, 11, and 16—direct or authorize the judge to impose sanctions on attorneys or parties or both if, for example, papers filed are not well grounded in fact and supported by a reasonable argument of law. Judges differ in their propensity to impose sanctions and in their view of the proper severity of sanctions. The law clerk should be familiar with the rules regarding sanctions and with the jurisprudence of the circuit court of appeals concerning their interpretation and application.

P. Trial

Chambers staff often do not attend trials because they are engaged in activities relating to the case or to other matters that require their attention. However, a law clerk may be called on to attend a trial and perform one or more of the following duties:

- Assist in jury selection (see *infra* section 5-3.D for more information on jury selection and management);

- Check the case file before trial to ensure that all necessary documents are present;

- Serve as court crier;

- Act as a messenger for the judge;

- Take notes of the testimony;

- Perform research on matters that arise during the course of the trial;

- Assist in the preparation of jury instructions; and

- In nonjury cases, assist in drafting findings of fact and conclusions of law.

Trials offer valuable experience for law clerks, and most judges encourage their clerks to attend interesting and skillfully presented trials when this does not interfere with their other responsibilities. A convenient alternative is for the court to have a transmitter connecting the courtroom microphones to the law clerk's office so the law clerk can listen when time is available.

Q. Post-Trial Motions and Enforcement of Judgments

Most post-trial motions involve attacks on the verdict or the judgment and are governed by specific provisions in the Federal Rules of Civil Procedure. Included are the following:

- Motion for new trial (Rule 59);

- Motion to alter or amend a judgment (Rule 59(e));

- Renewal of motion for judgment after trial (Rule 50(b)); and

- Motion for relief from a judgment on the ground of

  - clerical mistake (Rule 60(a));

  - other mistake (Rule 60(b));

  - inadvertence (Rule 60(b));

  - surprise (Rule 60(b));

  - excusable neglect (Rule 60(b));

  - newly discovered evidence (Rule 60(b));

  - fraud (Rule 60(b));

  - void judgment (Rule 60(b)); or

  - satisfaction, release, or discharge (Rule 60(b)).

These motions are processed like pretrial motions. The judge may prefer to handle them without oral argument, however, because of familiarity with the issue from earlier proceedings.

The procedures for execution and for supplementary proceedings in aid of judgment and execution are generally those of the state in which the court sits. Fed. R. Civ. P. 69. The following are the most common procedures:

- Execution;

- Attachment;

- Garnishment;

- Sequestration;

- Proceedings against sureties; and

- Contempt.

During the course of these proceedings the court may be called on to conduct evidentiary hearings, rule on motions, and supervise discovery in the same manner as during the original litigation on the merits.

R. Social Security Appeals

Some districts are presented with a large volume of appeals from the decisions of administrative agencies, and have created special procedures to handle them. An example is petitions for review of adverse decisions of the Social Security Administration (SSA). Some judges refer these to magistrate judges. Others handle these cases themselves with the assistance of law clerks. Typically, these cases concern eligibility for Social Security Disability Insurance Benefits or Supplemental Security Income Benefits (SSI). The former are awarded only when a claimant with a sufficient number of quarters of insured employment has suffered a mental or physical impairment such that he or she cannot perform substantial gainful employment for at least a year. The latter are awarded when the income and assets of a disabled person drop below a certain level and the person is not eligible for Disability Insurance Benefits.

If the SSA rejects a claim for such benefits, the claimant may obtain a hearing before an administrative law judge (ALJ) at which the ALJ questions the claimant (who may be represented by counsel) and any witnesses, and examines the records and medical or financial reports furnished by the claimant or the SSA. There is no advocate for the SSA at this hearing; the ALJ serves a function similar to that of an investigating magistrate in a European court. The ALJ writes an opinion—if the claim is denied, the claimant may appeal to the SSA Appeals Council, the last resort within the administrative system. If the appeals council denies a hearing or affirms the ALJ, "the decision of the secretary" (as it is called) is final and may be appealed to the district court within sixty days.

District court review is statutorily limited to a deferential examination of the record to determine whether adequate procedures were followed, whether the SSA relied on correct legal standards, and whether substantial evidence supports the administrative decision.

After a claimant files a petition, which may be in short form, the U.S. attorney's office supplies the court with the administrative record and an answer. Most districts have a general procedural order for the review procedure in such cases. This order requires the assistant U.S. attorney (AUSA) to file a motion for summary judgment to affirm the secretary's decision. The claimant may file a reply brief within a period fixed by the local rules, and the matter is then automatically taken under submission without oral argument, unless the judge orders otherwise.

Once the matter is under submission, the law clerk must write a draft order or opinion affirming the SSA's decision (the most common result because of the limited scope of review), reversing it, or remanding it either for a new hearing (because of a procedural or legal error) or to take new evidence.

The law clerk should obtain sample opinions rendered by the judge in other Social Security cases and use them as models. Lance Liebman, in *Disability Appeals in Social Security Programs* (Federal Judicial Center 1985), describes the Social Security Disability and Supplemental Security Income systems and the legal issues that frequently arise on judicial review of agency decisions.

S. Appeals

The basic steps in the appeal of a judgment are discussed in section 3-4 *infra*.

§ 3-2. The Criminal Action

In federal law there are no common-law crimes, only statutory offenses. Most federal crimes are defined in Titles 18 and 21 of the U.S. Code, but some criminal penalties are set forth in various other specific statutes. The procedure in criminal cases is governed by the

Federal Rules of Criminal Procedure; misdemeanor cases are governed by Federal Rule of Criminal Procedure 58. Much of the law clerk's involvement in criminal cases is similar to that described earlier for civil cases.

The following materials outline the major stages in a criminal case. This outline is only a generalization to aid in understanding the process. Individual cases may proceed in a different manner, and cases can terminate at various stages, such as when a guilty plea is entered by the defendant, the court grants a motion to dismiss the indictment, or the jury finds the defendant not guilty.

A. Proceedings Before a Magistrate Judge

A criminal case may begin in any of the following ways:

- Arrest without warrant followed by

  - filing of a complaint (Fed. R. Crim. P. 3);

  - appearance before a magistrate judge (Fed. R. Crim. P. 5);

  - commitment or release on bail (18 U.S.C. §§ 3141–3151);

  - preliminary hearing before a magistrate judge (Fed. R. Crim. P. 5.1); and

  - grand jury presentment (Fed. R. Crim. P. 6).

- Arrest on warrant issued upon a complaint (Fed. R. Crim. P. 4) followed by

  - appearance before a magistrate judge;

  - commitment or release on bail;

  - preliminary hearing before a magistrate judge; and

  - grand jury indictment (Fed. R. Crim. P. 6).

- Arrest on warrant issued upon indictment (Fed. R. Crim. P. 9) followed by

  - appearance before a magistrate judge; and

  - commitment or release on bail.

- Issuance of summons (Fed. R. Crim. P. 9), which directs the defendant to appear without being arrested.

Upon arrest a defendant must be brought before a magistrate judge "without unnecessary delay." Federal Rule of Criminal Procedure 5 requires that, at the first appearance before the magistrate judge, the defendant must be advised of the following:

- The charges contained in the complaint or the indictment and the content of any affidavits filed with the complaint;

- The defendant's right to retain counsel;

- The defendant's right to have counsel appointed if he or she is financially unable to retain counsel;

- The defendant's right to a preliminary hearing;

- The fact that the defendant is not required to make a statement and that, if the defendant does so, it may be used against him or her.

The magistrate judge may take the following additional actions:

- If the defendant cannot afford to retain counsel, appoint counsel unless the defendant declines the assistance of counsel (18 U.S.C. § 3006A(b));

- Determine bail or other conditions for release (18 U.S.C. § 3142); and

- If the defendant is unable to post bail or meet the conditions for release established by the magistrate judge, commit the defendant to custody (18 U.S.C. § 3142(e)).

B. Indictment

The Fifth Amendment guarantees a person charged with a serious federal crime the right to have the charge presented to a grand jury.

Grand juries are impaneled by the district court as needed. A grand jury consists of not fewer than sixteen nor more than twenty-three members, selected in accordance with the jury selection plan of the district court. Fed. R. Crim. P. 6. The jury continues to serve until discharged by the court, but it may not serve for more than eighteen months.

Rule 6(c) states that the court "shall appoint one of the jurors to be foreperson and another to be deputy foreperson." The foreperson is responsible for recording the number of jurors concurring in the finding on each indictment and for filing that record with the clerk of court.

Grand jury proceedings are usually secret, but the court can direct disclosure. Fed. R. Crim. P. 6(e). Government counsel, the witness, and necessary court reporters and interpreters may be present while evidence is being presented, but only the jurors themselves may be present during deliberation and voting. Grand jury indictments are presented to a judge or magistrate judge in open court.

A defendant who is entitled to be prosecuted by indictment may waive that right in open court. In that case, prosecution is by bill of information. Fed. R. Crim. P. 7(b).

C. Arraignment

The purpose of arraignment is to frame the issues between the prosecution and the defense. The defendant may plead guilty, not guilty, or nolo contendere. The court may refuse to accept a plea of guilty or nolo contendere. If the defendant pleads guilty or nolo contendere, the court must be satisfied that the defendant understands the nature of the charge, the maximum and minimum mandatory penalties, and that the plea is made voluntarily. Fed. R. Crim. P. 11(c) and (d). Some judges also ask questions to satisfy themselves that defendants accused of crimes committed after October 1987 understand that the Sentencing Reform Act applies and that, therefore, the Sentencing Guidelines will likely be used to determine the sentence. (For more information on sentencing, see *infra* section 3-2.H.)

At the time of arraignment, the defendant will usually plead not guilty. This gives counsel time to research the legal rules governing the charges, investigate the evidence against the client, ascertain whether any of the evidence may be suppressed, and determine whether a plea bargain is desirable or possible. Thereafter, a plea of guilty or nolo contendere is frequently entered as a result of plea bargaining between the prosecution and the defense. Plea bargaining is a process through which the defendant agrees to enter a guilty plea on the condition that the prosecution reduce the charge, dismiss some of a group of multiple charges, or grant some other concession. The judge must inquire of a defendant whether there has been any agreement or plea bargain and, if so, the understanding or agreement must be fully set forth in the record. Fed. R. Crim. P. 11(e). In the federal court system the judge is not a party to the plea bargaining process and is not bound by any agreement made between the defendant and the government. For defendants subject to the Sentencing Guidelines, judges may accept the plea agreement on a conditional basis, pending determination of the guideline sentence. Only with that determination can the court know whether the sentence contemplated by the plea agreement accords with the sentence allowed under the guidelines.

If the defendant pleads not guilty and does not thereafter change the plea, the case proceeds to trial.

D. Pretrial Motions

Motions are most frequently filed before trial for the following reasons:

- To challenge the sufficiency of the indictment or information, by way of a motion to dismiss;

- To challenge the jurisdiction or venue;

- To suppress evidence, usually on the ground that it was obtained in a manner that violated the defendant's constitutional rights;

- To discover evidence;

- When the defendant is indigent:

    - to request that specialized services such as psychiatric examination, special investigations, or expert services be provided at the expense of the United States;

    - to obtain the appointment of counsel if this has not already been done; and

- To obtain release of the defendant on reduced bail or the defendant's own recognizance while awaiting trial.

Motions are sometimes filed late in the proceedings. For example, a motion for severance of a trial from the trial of a codefendant may be filed three or four days before the pretrial conference, which may be set only a week or two before trial. The assistant U.S. attorney charged with the prosecution of the case may not respond until the pretrial conference. Therefore, when a motion is filed in a criminal case, it usually requires prompt attention, and often the law clerk will brief the judge orally or write a memo summarizing the motion and the law on the subject before the opposition papers are filed.

E. Discovery and Pretrial Omnibus Hearing

Traditionally, discovery in criminal cases has been extremely limited. However, Federal Rule of Criminal Procedure 16 permits the defendant to discover some of the evidentiary material in the government's possession. If the defendant does seek discovery under Rule 16, the government is entitled to a limited amount of discovery in return. The matters that are subject to such discovery are set forth specifically in that rule.

Many courts conduct a pretrial hearing to determine what motions will be filed, to simplify issues, and to expedite disclosure of the government's evidence. This so-called omnibus hearing is designed to combine all discovery procedures and motions. Proponents believe that these hearings ensure that the defendant has asserted all possible rights and defenses, avoid last-minute motions, streamline the trial, and eliminate some trials that would be conducted only because counsel is unaware of the government's evidence. Some districts refer to the hearing by the number of the local rule concerning it, for example, a Rule 2.04 hearing. The law clerk should inquire whether the court has such a rule and, if it does, should become familiar with it.

F. Trial and Post-Trial Detention

The jury in a criminal case consists of twelve jurors and as many alternates as the court thinks necessary. At trial, the jury is impaneled, evidence is presented, and a verdict is rendered by the jury. If the verdict is "guilty," the court must decide whether to alter the custody of the defendant pending sentencing and must set a date to impose sentence. If the defendant is not in custody, the judge will usually inquire whether the defendant should be at large on the same bond, pending imposition of sentence. The Bail Reform Act of 1984 requires that a person found guilty and awaiting imposition of sentence must be detained unless the judge finds "by clear and convincing evidence that the person is not likely to flee or pose a danger to the safety of any other person or the community" if released. 18 U.S.C. § 3143(a). A presentence investigation will usually be ordered. The defendant either is notified to appear for sentencing on a fixed date or is informed that the court will give notice by mail of the date sentence is to be imposed.

G. The Speedy Trial Act

According to its preamble, the Speedy Trial Act of 1974 (18 U.S.C. §§ 3161–3174) was enacted "to assist in reducing crime and the danger of recidivism by requiring speedy trials and by strengthening the supervision over persons released pending trial." That act has an important impact on proceedings in criminal cases. It requires each district to adopt a plan for the disposition of criminal cases. District court law clerks and secretaries should become thoroughly familiar with both the Act and the local court plan.

The administration of the criminal trial calendar is vested in the court. The Act requires the court "at the earliest practicable time . . . after consultation with the counsel for the defendant and the attorney for the Government" to set the case for trial "on a day certain, or list it for trial on a weekly or other short-term trial calendar." 18 U.S.C. § 3161(a).

The prosecutor must file an information or indictment within thirty days of arrest or service of summons. 18 U.S.C. § 3161(b). An additional thirty days is allowed if no grand jury has met in the district within the first thirty-day period. Then commences an inexorable movement toward trial. Further time limits are prescribed in section 3161.

There are eight exclusions for delays that will not violate speedy trial requirements. These include the following:

- Mental or physical examination (18 U.S.C. § 3161(h)(1)(A));

- Hearings on pretrial motions (18 U.S.C. § 3161(h)(1)(F));

- Period not to exceed thirty days during which the judge has a matter concerning the defendant under advisement (18 U.S.C. § 3161(h)(1)(J));

- Period during which prosecution is deferred by written agreement with the defendant, with the approval of the court, for the purpose of allowing the defendant to demonstrate his good conduct (18 U.S.C. § 3161(h)(2));

- Periods when the defendant or an essential witness is absent or unavailable or is mentally incapable (18 U.S.C. § 3161(h)(3)(A), (h)(4)); and

- Delay resulting from a continuance issued by a judge on the court's own motion or that of counsel, if the continuance was granted based on the judge's findings that the ends of justice served by the delay outweighed the public and the defendant's interest in a speedy trial (18 U.S.C. § 3161(h)(8)(A)).

No continuance can be granted because of court congestion, lack of diligent preparation, or failure to obtain witnesses on the part of the government.

Failure to meet prescribed time limits requires dismissal of the charge. 18 U.S.C. § 3162. Whether the dismissal is with or without prejudice is to be determined by the court after considering the following:

- The seriousness of the offense;

- The facts and circumstances of the case that led to dismissal; and

- The impact of a reprosecution on the administration of the Act and on the administration of justice generally.

The Act authorizes sanctions against counsel, for both the defendant and the government, if they

- Knowingly allow a case to be set for trial without disclosing the unavailability of a necessary witness;

- File a motion that they know is frivolous;

- Knowingly make a materially false statement to obtain a continuance; or

- Otherwise willfully fail to proceed to trial without justification.

The maximum penalties are fixed by the Act.

H. Sentencing

(*Note:* This material applies to offenses committed on or after November 1, 1987, the effective date of the Sentencing Reform Act of 1984 described below. Offenses committed before November 1, 1987, are not subject to the Act, and the judge has considerably more discretion as to the sentence to impose. The presentence report prepared for such offenses will be much different from the report described below.)

1. Sources

Sentencing and sentencing procedures in federal court are controlled by four main sources: the statutory maximums and minimums prescribed for the offenses in Titles 18 and 21 and other sections of the U.S. Code; the Sentencing Reform Act of 1984 and various subsequent amending statutes; the federal Sentencing Guidelines that are set forth in the *Guidelines Manual* issued by the U.S. Sentencing Commission pursuant to the Sentencing Reform Act; and the Federal Rules of Criminal Procedure, especially Rule 32 ("Sentence and Judgment") and Rule 35 ("Correction or Reduction of Sentence").

Each judge's chambers has a copy of the Commission's *Guidelines Manual.* An appendix to this manual includes the sections of Titles 18 and 28 enacted by the Sentencing Reform Act (note, however, that this is not an authoritative version of the legislation). Law clerks may also wish to consult the Federal Judicial Center's *Guideline Sentencing Update,* a loose-leaf series summarizing developments in guideline sentencing case law, and *Guideline Sentencing. An Outline of Appellate Case Law on Selected Issues,* a cumulative outline of guidelines-related appellate case law. Other instructional material that the Center or the Commission may distribute should also be kept on hand.

In the 1984 Sentencing Reform Act, Congress attempted to reduce unwarranted disparity in sentencing and ensure that similar defendants who commit similar crimes receive similar sentences. There was also concern that defendants' actual sentences were in effect determined by a parole commission rather than the court. Consequently, Congress created the U.S. Sentencing Commission as a permanent agency in the judicial branch and directed it to promulgate sentencing guidelines and amendments to the guidelines, which take effect absent congressional action.

The Sentencing Guidelines—strictly defined and identified as such in the *Guidelines Manual*—have the force of law. The Sentencing Reform Act also authorized the Commission to issue "policy statements" to explain the guidelines and their application. In its guidelines document, the Commission has also provided "commentary" and application notes, which further explain the guidelines and the Commission's intent. With occasional exceptions, policy statements and commentary must be followed by the court. At the time of sentencing, the court must state in open court the reasons for its imposition of the particular sentence. If it imposes a sentence "not of the kind" or "outside the range" prescribed by the guidelines, the court must state "the specific reason" for not following the guidelines. 18 U.S.C. § 3553(c). Either the defendant or the government may appeal a sentence imposed as a result of an incorrect application of the guidelines. 18 U.S.C. § 3742.

Pursuant to the Sentencing Reform Act, the Commission established numerous categories of offense conduct to which it assigned levels according to the seriousness of the offense. The levels are to be adjusted based on particular characteristics of the offense (such as use of a weapon), so that the sentence reflects the "total offense conduct," not simply the offense charged in the indictment. Also pursuant to statute, the Commission established criminal history categories, based on the number and seriousness of a defendant's prior offenses. A defendant's sentencing range, in months, is based on the combination of offense level and criminal history category. However, if a statutory mandatory minimum sentence applies to an offense, and the guideline sentence is lower than the mandatory minimum, the mandatory minimum sentence must be used.

The judge must impose a sentence within the range prescribed by the guidelines unless "the court finds that there exists an aggravating or mitigating circumstance of a kind, or to a degree, that was not adequately taken into consideration by the Sentencing Commission in formulating the guidelines that should result in a sentence different from that described." In making a finding about what the Commission considered, the court may "consider only the sentencing guidelines, policy statements, and official commentary of the Sentencing Commission." 18 U.S.C. § 3553(b). If it does make such a finding, the court may depart from the sentence prescribed by the guidelines.

The sentence imposed will be the length of time actually to be served, except that fifty-four days of good time credit may be earned each year after the first year. The guidelines also tell how to determine the fine to be imposed in addition to any statutorily required restitution, and they indicate when probation or some other sentence instead of incarceration may be imposed. Although the Sentencing Reform Act does not provide for parole, the sentence may include a term of supervised release to follow the prison sentence.

2. Sentencing Procedures

In most courts, the basic document the judge uses to determine the sentence is the presentence report prepared by a probation officer. Federal Rule of Criminal Procedure 32(c)(2) prescribes the contents of the presentence report. The report presents the facts of the case relevant to guideline sentencing, explains the results of the officer's application of the guidelines to them, and provides the officer's confidential sentencing recommendation. It may contain an addendum listing statements in the report to which one of the parties objects and also the officer's comments on those objections. The Probation and Pretrial Services Division of the Administrative Office has suggested a standard format for presentence reports and has prepared a document explaining it. The court's probation office can provide general information about the report and its preparation.

18 U.S.C. § 3552(d) requires disclosure of the presentence report to the defendant at least ten days before sentencing. Some courts have local rules that provide for disclosure of the presentence report twenty or more days in advance of sentencing. The purpose of this longer time period is to allow the attorneys to review the report and discuss their objections with the probation officer. The probation officer can revise the report to take account of legitimate objections and summarize and comment on unresolved objections in an addendum to the revised presentence report. Some courts have adopted local rules that do not inject the probation officer so extensively into the fact-finding process. They direct the parties to file a motion or memorandum discussing unresolved issues directly with the court.

If there are disputed factual issues that could affect the sentence, the judge may find it necessary to hold an evidentiary hearing before imposing a sentence. (The Federal Rules of Evidence do not apply at the sentencing hearing.) In addition, if there is a dispute concerning the correct interpretation of the guidelines, the court may wish to hear argument from the attorneys. After resolving the disputes, the judge imposes sentence. 18 U.S.C. § 3553(c) requires the court to state the reasons for the sentence on the record in order to facilitate appellate review. It also requires that a statement of reasons be furnished to the probation office and, if the sentence includes imprisonment, to the Bureau of Prisons.

3. Appellate Review

Either the defendant or the government may appeal the sentence on the ground that it was imposed in violation of law or represents an incorrect application of the guidelines. Also, guideline departures are appealable by the defendant if the sentence is above the guidelines, or by the government if it is below. If the appeals court reverses the sentence, the case is remanded to the district court for resentencing, unless the same sentence would have been imposed absent the invalid factors. Federal Rule of Criminal Procedure 35 requires the court, upon remand, to correct a sentence determined on appeal to have been improperly imposed. However, Rule 35, as amended, no longer gives the judge authority in other circumstances to reopen the sentence, even if it is illegal, except that the government may petition for a reduction in reward for cooperation. The one exception is Rule 35(c), effective December 1, 1991, which gives a court seven days to "correct a sentence that was imposed as a result of arithmetical, technical, or other clear error." Before Rule 35(c), some circuits held that district courts retained inherent discretion to correct illegal sentences in particular situations—law clerks should check the law of their circuit.

4. Role of Law Clerks

District judges vary as to what they require of their law clerks in respect to sentencing. Law clerks who are asked to review the presentence report to assess the correctness of the probation officer's guidelines application will have to become thoroughly familiar with the Commission's *Guidelines Manual* and guidelines case law in their circuit. The guidelines, policy statements, and commentary can be quite complex and sometimes yield more than one plausible interpretation. Simply consulting the guideline for the type of offense in question will rarely produce a correct offense-level determination. A correct determination will also reflect, for example, how much of the offender's actual conduct should be taken into account in applying the specific offense characteristics. One must, moreover, be familiar with the entire structure of the guidelines in order to apply them to any particular case. Sample sentencing worksheets prepared by the Commission are found as an appendix in the *Federal Sentencing Guidelines Manual,* distributed by West Publishing Company.

The law clerk also should pay special attention to the effective dates for the relevant legislative and guideline provisions to ascertain which provisions apply to the offense in question.

Some judges may wish their law clerks to draft a tentative statement of reasons for the sentence. Bear in mind that the sentence, and thus the statement of reasons, may depend on the resolution of disputed issues of law or fact; these issues may appear in the addendum to the presentence report or may be raised at the sentencing hearing.

Just before the sentencing date, the law clerk or secretary should assemble the court files needed for the sentencings set for that day. These should be placed in a convenient place in chambers so that the judge may, if he or she chooses to do so, reexamine the files just before the sentencing hearing. The files should be placed on the bench just before court is called to order.

I. Post-Trial Motions

The usual post-trial motions in a criminal case are for a new trial, for arrest of judgment, or to correct or reduce the sentence. The court's authority to correct or reduce the sentence is limited under Federal Rule of Criminal Procedure 35. Post-trial motions are generally processed in the same manner as other motions. Motions under 28 U.S.C. § 2255 are discussed in the next section.

J. Handling Prisoner Petitions

Federal courts receive many petitions from prison inmates requesting relief from their sentences or protesting their conditions of confinement. The majority of petitions are from state prisoners alleging violation by state officials of the prisoners' federally protected procedural rights, and seeking release from state custody under the federal habeas corpus act, 28 U.S.C. § 2254. These are to be distinguished from petitions seeking damages or injunctive relief for violation of a prisoner's civil rights under 42 U.S.C. § 1983. Both section 2254 and section 1983 actions are civil proceedings.

Federal prisoners may seek release from custody under 28 U.S.C. § 2255. Although section 2255 is similar to habeas corpus, it requires the petition to be filed in the sentencing court rather than in the court having jurisdiction over the place of incarceration (a section 2255 proceeding is considered a continuation of the original criminal action). This eliminates problems of transferring case files and usually permits ready access to witnesses and other evidence.

Prisoner petitions are frequently handwritten and unartfully drafted. As a result, they may be difficult to read and understand. The rules governing cases under section 2254 and section 2255 are available in pamphlet form from the Administrative Office and may be found in the *United States Code Annotated* following the statutory sections. Pro se petitioners in such cases must complete a standard form in order to make the alleged facts and the nature of the claim more intelligible. The Administrative Office provides forms AO-241, AO-242, AO-243, and AO-244. These forms are mandatory in pro se cases, but district courts may amend them to meet local requirements. The forms assist prisoners and the court by ensuring that critical information is provided in a coherent format. In a further attempt to process the large volume of prisoner petitions, some courts have created the position of motions law clerk or pro se law clerk. Some district courts also have standard forms for use as pro se petitions based on section 1983. (Additional discussion of prisoner correspondence can be found at section 7-2.G.3 *infra*.)

Judges can decide many of the post-conviction petitions by examining the papers, but if material factual issues are raised, the court must conduct an evidentiary hearing.

K. Suggested Reference Material

Bench Book for United States District Court Judges (3d ed. Federal Judicial Center 1986)

Introducing the Federal Courts, Program 2: How Criminal Cases Move Through the District Courts (Federal Judicial Center 1991) (five videocassettes)

§ 3-3. Bankruptcy

A. General Structure

Each judicial district has a bankruptcy court, which constitutes a unit of the district court (28 U.S.C. § 151), and to which bankruptcy cases and proceedings may be referred (28 U.S.C. § 157(a)). In almost all districts, the administration of the bankruptcy court is directed by a separate clerk. In a few districts, the clerk of the district court also serves as clerk of the bankruptcy court. The functions of the bankruptcy clerk's office are similar to those of the clerk of the district court.

Bankruptcy judges are appointed by the court of appeals for a term of fourteen years and may be removed from office only for incompetence, misconduct, neglect of duty, or physical or mental disability, and then only by the circuit judicial council. If the district has more than one bankruptcy judge, judges of the district court designate a chief judge. Each bankruptcy judge is entitled to a staff, including a secretary and a law clerk.

The bankruptcy laws are codified in two places in the U.S. Code. Title 28, the Judicial Code, contains the provisions on bankruptcy jurisdiction, bankruptcy judges and the "bankruptcy court," venue and transfer, and the structure of the U.S. trustee system. Title 11, the Bankruptcy Code, contains both substantive and procedural law for bankruptcy proceedings. The Bankruptcy Code was adopted by the Bankruptcy Reform Act of 1978 and has been amended by (1) the Federal Judgeship Act of 1984, the bankruptcy section of which was passed primarily to remedy constitutional defects in the Code's provisions for the jurisdiction of bankruptcy courts following the decision in *Northern Pipeline Const. Co. v. Marathon Pipe Line Co.*, 458 U.S. 50 (1982); and (2) the Family Farmer Bankruptcy Act of 1986, 11 U.S.C. § 1201–1231.

Federal courts have original and exclusive jurisdiction of all cases under the Bankruptcy Code; a bankruptcy case may not be filed in a state court. The district courts also have original, but not exclusive, jurisdiction over "all civil proceedings arising under Title 11, or arising in or related to cases under Title 11." 28 U.S.C. § 1334(b). These phrases—"proceedings arising under Title 11" and "arising in or related to cases under Title 11"—are terms of art. A "case" refers to the entire matter relating to a particular debtor. A "proceeding" is any disputed matter arising in the course of a case. Thus a single case may present many proceedings. By creating the bankruptcy jurisdictional scheme, Congress intended to eliminate the litigation over jurisdiction that occurred under the former Bankruptcy Act.

The definition of the terms "arising under," "arising in," and "related to" and the distinctions among them are complex. A helpful discussion is found in *Collier on Bankruptcy* (15th ed.). A number of shorter and simpler books on bankruptcy are cited at the end of this section.

Because federal jurisdiction over civil *proceedings* is nonexclusive, other federal and state courts are not deprived of jurisdiction over matters to which bankruptcy jurisdiction extends. It is frequently desirable to permit bankruptcy litigation to proceed elsewhere even though the bankruptcy court has jurisdiction to hear it. Thus, the district court or the bankruptcy court may, for various reasons, choose (or may occasionally be required) to abstain from hearing a particular proceeding, may remand an action removed to it, or may authorize an action to be filed originally in some other court.

Federal bankruptcy jurisdiction, even when nonexclusive, is paramount. Litigation in other courts is generally stayed automatically by the filing of a bankruptcy petition under Bankruptcy Code § 362, or may be enjoined by an affirmative injunction issued under Bankruptcy Code § 105(a). Actions in other courts may be removed to the district court sitting in bankruptcy. 28 U.S.C. § 1452. The decision to abstain, remand, or not remand a removed action is not reviewable. 28 U.S.C. §§ 1334(c)(2), 1452(b).

Abstention in a civil proceeding ordinarily is discretionary with the federal court. The discretion is guided by the flexible "interest of justice" standard or "comity with State courts or respect for State law." 28 U.S.C. § 1334(c)(1). When the lawsuit is a traditional matter for the civil courts or involves issues about which bankruptcy judges lack special expertise, the district court may decide to abstain, particularly if the litigation would be lengthy, the bankruptcy court's regular calendar is crowded, and a reasonably prompt disposition by the state court could be expected.

In certain limited situations, abstention is mandatory if a timely motion is made. The court must abstain if the proceeding is a "related" proceeding; is based on a cause of action created by state law; does not "arise in" or "arise under" Title 11; is commenced in state court; or can be timely adjudicated in a state forum of appropriate jurisdiction, and there is no diversity or federal question jurisdiction.

Whether jury trials are contemplated in bankruptcy cases and proceedings is barely treated by the Bankruptcy Code. The right to a jury trial in the district court is explicitly preserved for specified tort claims (non-core proceedings) brought by the estate or asserted against the estate for distribution purposes only. 28 U.S.C. §§ 157(b)(2)(B), 157(b)(5), 1411(a). Prior to a 1989 Supreme Court opinion, some courts concluded that there was no constitutional right to a jury trial in core proceedings. But in *Granfinanciera, S.A. v. Nordberg*, 492 U.S. 33 (1989), the Court cast considerable doubt on this position, holding that the Seventh Amendment ensured a jury trial to set aside an alleged fraudulent transfer, notwithstanding Congress' designation of fraudulent conveyance actions as core proceedings in 28 U.S.C. § 157(b)(2)(H). Even if a right to a jury trial exists in certain proceedings, it is unresolved whether bankruptcy courts are empowered to conduct a jury trial themselves or whether any jury trial must be conducted by the district court.

B. Reference to Bankruptcy Court

The district court in which a bankruptcy case is commenced has exclusive jurisdiction of the bankruptcy case and of all property of the debtor, wherever located, as of the commencement of the case. As noted above, the district court also has concurrent jurisdiction over "proceedings" that "arise in," "arise under," or are "related to" the proceeding. Pursuant to 28 U.S.C. § 157(a), the district courts are authorized to refer to the bankruptcy judges for the district any or all cases under Title 11 and all proceedings that arise in, arise under, or are related to these cases.

Each district court has a standing order referring all bankruptcy cases and proceedings to the bankruptcy court. The district court may, however, decide not to refer a specific case or proceeding or, after having referred it, may withdraw the reference. Sometimes a district judge may decide to sit with a bankruptcy judge in handling particularly significant cases.

Bankruptcy judges may enter a final order in all "*core proceedings arising under Title 11*," but not in "*non-core proceedings*"; the latter term simply refers to all matters that are not "core" proceedings (emphasis added). As the phrase itself implies, "core proceeding" describes matters that are at the heart of the bankruptcy case (except that, even when they affect the assets of the estate, personal-injury and wrongful-death tort claims must be tried by the district court). The phrase is defined specifically, albeit not inclusively, in 28 U.S.C. § 157(b)(2), which contains a nonexclusive list of fifteen items that are core proceedings.

The Code contains no express definition of a non-core proceeding. One example is an in personae cause of action, not created by the Code, that the debtor possessed at the time of the petition and that became a part of the estate as a result of the filing of the case. Another is a suit between third parties to which neither the debtor nor the estate is a party but which is within the broad jurisdictional grant because it indirectly affects the estate, such as a suit by a creditor against a guarantor of the debtor's obligation.

The bankruptcy judge determines initially whether a particular matter is core. Unless the parties by consent give the bankruptcy judge authority to enter final orders and judgments in a non-core matter, the bankruptcy judge must submit proposed findings of fact and conclusions of law in such matters to the district court. Bankruptcy judges may assign to their law clerks the preparation of drafts of such findings and conclusions. After considering the bankruptcy judge's proposed findings and conclusions, and after reviewing de novo those matters to which any party has timely and specifically objected, the district court enters the final judgment.

Appeals from final judgments, orders, and decrees of the bankruptcy court in core proceedings are taken to the district courts. The district court also has discretion to review interlocutory appeals. A circuit judicial council may establish a Bankruptcy Appellate Panel (BAP) consisting of three bankruptcy judges. If the circuit judicial council creates such a panel, a majority of the district judges for the district authorize appeals from the district to go to the BAP, and the parties consent, then the BAP may hear appeals from bankruptcy judge decisions. Further appeals from both district court and BAP decisions are taken to the circuit court of appeals.

Because appeals from bankruptcy courts are taken first to district courts (or to BAPs) and then to courts of appeals, it is important for law clerks in all federal courts to understand the bankruptcy court structure. Most bankruptcy practice is handled by specialists who may assume that everyone else is familiar with the bankruptcy system.

The Code relieves the bankruptcy judge of administrative and ministerial functions to allow the judge to focus on essentially judicial functions. Administrative matters in a bankruptcy case are performed by the office of the U.S. Trustee, as discussed below.

C. The Bankruptcy Code

The Bankruptcy Code's first three chapters contain provisions of general applicability. Chapter 1 contains definitions, rules of construction, and other general rules. Chapter 3 describes how a case is begun (voluntary and involuntary petitions); deals with officers and their compensation; and contains various administrative provisions and administrative powers, including provisions concerning the automatic stay (section 362), the use, sale, and lease of property (section 363), and the assumption or rejection of executory contracts (section 365). Chapter 5 contains much of the substantive bankruptcy law concerning creditors, debtors, and the estate.

The provisions of Chapters 1, 3, and 5 apply in any kind of case under the Bankruptcy Code, whether it be liquidation under Chapter 7 or rehabilitation under Chapter 11, 12, or 13. Chapter 9 contains its own section (section 901) specifying which provisions in the other chapters apply in a Chapter 9 case. In contrast, the provisions found in Chapters 7, 9, 11, 12, and 13 apply only to cases brought under each particular chapter.

Chapter 7 relates to liquidation proceedings or "straight bankruptcy." Its purpose is to achieve a fair distribution to creditors of whatever nonexempt property the debtor has and to give the individual debtor a fresh start through the discharge in bankruptcy. It requires the appointment of a trustee whose sole function is to collect and liquidate the debtor's assets in order to generate cash for distribution to creditors. If the debtor has complied with applicable law, the debtor will receive a discharge of all dischargeable debts. A creditor may, however, object to the discharge of the debtor or only to the discharge of a particular debt. The Code states the grounds on which such objections may be made. Liquidations of stockbrokers and commodity brokers are governed by a separate subchapter.

Chapter 9 relates to adjustment of the debts of municipalities and smaller government entities (such as water districts). It is invoked relatively infrequently.

Chapter 11, entitled "Reorganization," is the primary rehabilitation proceeding. It applies to debtors engaged in business, including individuals, partnerships, and corporations, whether publicly or closely held. The goal of Chapter 11 cases ordinarily is to rehabilitate a business as a going concern rather than to liquidate it. Unless a trustee is appointed by the court, the debtor is allowed to remain in possession (as a "debtor-in-possession" or "DIP") of its property. The chapter's purpose is to give the debtor a fresh start through the binding effect of an order confirming a plan of reorganization, after full disclosure to all interested persons.

Chapter 12 was adopted in 1986 and is scheduled to expire in 1998. The chapter provides for the adjustment of the debts of a family farmer with regular income. Chapter 12 plans are more similar to Chapter 13 plans than to Chapter 11 reorganizations. As is the situation under Chapter 13, but unlike Chapter 11, a discharge is not effective until all payments are made.

Chapter 13 is a rehabilitation provision for wage earners and other individuals with a regular income whose debts do not exceed specified amounts. Typically it is used to budget some of the debtor's future earnings under a plan through which all creditors are paid in whole or in part. The fresh start results from the discharge granted at the end of the case; the debtor's incentive to propose a plan rather than use Chapter 7 stems from the ability of the debtor to retain all property rather than turn it over to a trustee for liquidation and from the sometimes more favorable or broader discharge provisions found in Chapter 13. Chapter 13 is available only to individuals who meet the eligibility requirements set forth in section 109 of the Code.

D. Bankruptcy Rules

A case in bankruptcy court begins with the filing of a petition under the applicable chapter. If the debtor initiates the bankruptcy case, it is voluntary. Creditors may initiate involuntary cases, but only under Chapters 7 and 11. The petition is filed under the specific chapter of the code that governs the type of case contemplated. With limited exceptions, cases can generally be converted from one chapter to another.

The Federal Rules of Bankruptcy Procedure (RBP) govern cases in bankruptcy courts. Many of the rules are modeled on (and many even incorporate by reference) the Federal Rules of Civil Procedure. In addition, most districts have local bankruptcy rules governing some of the procedural aspects of bankruptcy cases. A law clerk for a bankruptcy judge should obtain a copy of both the RBP and the local bankruptcy rules in addition to the local district court rules and keep all of these readily available.

Certain types of proceedings within bankruptcy cases are called "adversary proceedings" and are governed and defined by RBP 7001–7087. Most matters in a bankruptcy case that do not qualify as adversary proceedings are called "contested matters."

The summons issued by the bankruptcy court clerk sets a date for either a trial or pretrial conference when a complaint in an adversary proceeding is filed. Contested matters are commenced by the filing of a motion. Local practice (usually set out in local rules) determines how motions are set for hearings. First class mail is usually used for service in adversary proceedings and contested matters. The rules regarding pleadings and discovery are similar to those in the Federal Rules of Civil Procedure.

When a bankruptcy petition is filed, all judicial proceedings in which the debtor is involved are automatically stayed. Thereafter, a variety of motions may be filed seeking some relief from the court. Relief will usually be granted after notice to other parties in interest if no one raises an objection. A typical motion is a motion for the abandonment of burdensome property.

Law clerks and secretaries for bankruptcy judges may be assigned the same tasks in connection with motions (whether ex parte or contested) that are assigned to law clerks and secretaries for district courts. The functions of the bankruptcy judges' law clerks in the trial of adversary proceedings are the same as those of district court law clerks in civil cases. *See supra* section 3-1.

E. U.S. Trustees and Private Trustees

The office of the United States Trustee (UST) handles the administrative functions of bankruptcy cases. Following an experimental program using U.S. trustees, in 1986 Congress adopted the program nationwide. The Bankruptcy Amendments Act of 1986 divided the United States into twenty-one geographic regions, in each of which a UST is responsible for bankruptcy administration. 28 U.S.C. § 581(a). The Attorney General appoints a UST to a five-year term. In addition, the Attorney General may appoint assistant U.S. Trustees when the public interest so requires. 28 U.S.C. § 582.

The duties of the UST, set forth at 28 U.S.C. § 586(a), include establishing a panel of private trustees eligible to serve as trustees in Chapter 7 liquidation cases (28 U.S.C. § 586(a)(1)) and serving as a trustee in Chapter 7 cases when a private trustee is not available (although a UST rarely does so) (28 U.S.C. § 586(a)(2)). In Chapter 11 cases, the UST appoints a private trustee if the court orders one, but the UST may not serve as a trustee in these cases. Private trustees are individuals appointed in a specific case to carry out the duties of a trustee in that case. In Chapters 12 and 13, the UST may act as trustee (although this is rarely done) or may appoint a private standing trustee. 28 U.S.C. § 586(b). The UST is also empowered, among other things, to monitor applications for employment and compensation for professionals; to monitor plans filed in reorganization cases; and to ensure that all required schedules and other papers are timely and properly filed and that fees are paid. 28 U.S.C. § 586(a)(3)(A)–(H). The UST, however, does not have independent enforcement powers; rather, it must request the court to rule on matters of administration as to which there is no voluntary compliance.

On approval by the Attorney General, the UST may employ a staff. 28 U.S.C. § 589. A set portion of fees is deposited into a U.S. Trustees System Fund to be used for salaries, benefits, and expenses of U.S. Trustees. Each judicial district has, with the approval of the Administrative Office, designated a number of persons with competence in bankruptcy matters to serve as trustees.

In a Chapter 7 case, when the petition is filed, the UST appoints a disinterested person from the panel of private trustees to serve as interim trustee. In an involuntary case, if the court orders the appointment of an interim trustee before the entry of the order for relief, the UST makes the appointment. At the first meeting of creditors, the creditors may elect another person as trustee, although such elections are rare.

In a Chapter 11 case, no trustee is appointed unless the court orders the appointment after notice and a hearing. If the court orders the appointment of a trustee, the UST designates the person who will serve.

In all Chapter 12 and Chapter 13 cases, a standing trustee (selected by the UST) serves; in a few districts there are several standing Chapter 12 or Chapter 13 trustees.

F. Suggested Reference Material

Collier on Bankruptcy (15th ed.) (a thirteen-volume treatise)

W. Homer Drake, Jr., Bankruptcy Practice for the General Practitioner (2d ed. 1990)

Harvey W. Lebowitz, Bankruptcy Deskbook (2d ed. 1990)

George M. Triester, et al., Fundamentals of Bankruptcy Law (2d ed. 1988)

Elizabeth Warren, Business Bankruptcy (Federal Judicial Center 1993)

Introducing the Federal Courts, Program 4: How Cases Move Through the Bankruptcy Courts (Federal Judicial Center 1994) (four videocassettes)

§ 3-4. Appeals

A. Processing Appeals

There are fewer steps in the appellate process than in the trial process. The steps in an appeal are as follows:

- Filing notice of appeal;

- Preparing the record on appeal;

- Docketing the appeal;

- Filing of appellant's brief;

- Filing of appellee's brief;

- Filing of appellant's reply brief;

- Decision by the court if it dispenses with oral argument, or scheduling of oral argument;

- Oral argument;

- Deliberation by court;

- Filing of opinion;

- Filing of petition for rehearing; and

- Issuance of mandate. (The mandate is the final stage in the appellate process unless the defendant applies to the Supreme Court for a writ of certiorari or files an appeal in those few instances in which appeals are permitted. *See, e.g.,* 28 U.S.C. §§ 1253, 1254.)

The Federal Rules of Appellate Procedure establish a certain degree of procedural uniformity among the thirteen courts of appeals. There are still, however, some differences in the procedures of the various circuits. Each circuit has local rules and internal operating procedures that describe the precise procedure to be followed when there is any variation from the rules and, in some instances, elaborate on or amplify the rules. *See infra* section 5-6.

B. Notice of Appeal

The timely filing of a notice of appeal is a jurisdictional requirement for any appeal. The purpose of the notice is to inform opposing counsel and the court that an appeal is being taken. The time for filing commences with the entry of the judgment or order in the district court from which the appeal is taken. The running of that time is tolled by the filing of certain post-trial motions in the district court, and the filing of such motions after a notice of appeal has been filed may vitiate the notice, requiring a new notice of appeal to be filed after the motion is decided. Fed. R. App. P. 4(a).

Rule 4 provides the following time periods for filing notices of appeal:

- Private civil cases—thirty days;

- Civil cases in which the United States is a party—sixty days;

- Criminal cases—ten days; and

- Criminal cases in which appeal by the government is authorized by statute (such as appeals from sentences under the 1984 Sentencing Reform Act)—thirty days.

The notice of appeal must be filed in the district court. The clerk of that court is required by Federal Rule of Appellate Procedure 3(d) to forward a copy of the notice to the clerk of the court of appeals.

Upon receipt of the notice of appeal, most courts of appeals take steps to ensure that all procedural requirements have been met and then monitor the appeal as it progresses in the district court. In some courts, conferences are held with counsel shortly after the notice is filed to establish schedules for record preparation and briefing, to discuss the issues in the case with a view to eliminating the briefing of frivolous issues, and, in civil cases, to discuss the possibility of settlement. Many circuits now require preargument conferences.

C. Record Preparation

For an appellate court to review intelligently the proceedings in a trial court, the appellate judges must have available a complete record of what occurred in the trial court. The appellant is required to cause a record on appeal to be filed. The record consists of all the original papers and exhibits filed in the trial court plus a reporter's transcript of any relevant proceedings. The Sentencing Reform Act (18 U.S.C. § 3742(d)) requires that the record in a criminal case must also include "(1) that portion of the record . . . that is designated as pertinent by either of the parties; (2) the presentence report; and (3) the information submitted during the sentencing proceeding." (This information will often be under seal because it is confidential.)

The appellant has forty days in which to cause the record on appeal to be sent from the district court to the court of appeals. During this time the appellant must order a transcript of proceedings if one is needed and make arrangements to pay the court reporter for services or, in courts using electronic sound recording for the official record, the clerk of court. The district court clerk assembles the other papers that constitute the record on appeal.

The district court has the power to extend for an additional fifty days the time for preparing and sending the record on appeal, after which the court of appeals itself may grant extensions. Additional time may be needed if the court reporter has not finished transcribing the proceedings or if counsel has failed to order the transcript in a timely manner.

To prevent undue delay, the appellate courts generally refuse to grant time extensions, and may impose sanctions on the appellant or the reporter for unreasonable delays in preparing the record on appeal.

D. Docketing the Appeal

When the record is completed, or earlier if desired, the appellant must docket the appeal. This is primarily a clerical process and is performed in the office of the Clerk of the Court of Appeals. Unless the appellant is exempt from payment, a docket fee is charged. The clerk of court opens an appropriate file and record, and sends a notice to the parties. Frequently, docketing takes place when the record on appeal is filed.

The filing of the record provides the base date for most subsequent proceedings in the case.

E. Briefs and Joint Appendix

Each party is given an opportunity to present legal and factual arguments to the court in writing. The document through which arguments are presented is the brief. Because the appellant has the burden of establishing that the trial court erred, it files the opening brief. The appellee then files a brief in response; if the appellant wishes, it may file a reply brief responding to new matters raised in the appellee's brief. The Federal Rules of Appellate Procedure establish standards for format, color of brief covers, content, methods of reproduction, number of copies, and times for filing of briefs. The local rules for a circuit may impose further requirements regarding the brief. The schedule for filing briefs is as follows:

- Appellant's brief—forty days after filing the record;

- Appellee's brief—thirty days after service of appellant's brief; and

- Reply brief—fourteen days after service of appellee's brief.

Some courts of appeals have modified the requirements and standards of the federal rules in certain cases or classes of cases. One of the more common modifications permits those appealing in forma pauperis to file fewer copies of their briefs.

While the briefs are being prepared, the parties are required to determine which portions of the record on appeal are relevant to the issues raised; the appellant must then have those portions reproduced as an appendix to the briefs. Since there is only one appendix containing the portions relied on by both the appellant and the appellee, it is referred to as a "joint appendix." If any relevant material is omitted from the appendix, the court is free to refer to the original record. Multiple copies of the appendix are filed so that each judge and, if needed, each law clerk may have one. Some courts of appeals have eliminated the requirement of an appendix and permit the substitution of photocopies of a relatively few parts of the record, usually called record excerpts. The local rules of those courts describe the substitute requirements.

F. Oral Argument

If the court does not decide a case exclusively on the basis of the briefs and written record, the parties are given an opportunity to present their arguments to the court orally. Federal Rule of Appellate Procedure 34 permits the court to fix the time allowed for oral argument. Most courts allow twenty minutes to each side, but some reduce this for cases that the panel thinks require less time. All courts allow counsel to file a request in advance for additional time, but such requests are not usually favored. Generally, not more than two attorneys are permitted to argue for each side. Some court rules encourage argument by only one attorney for each party.

Many circuit judges require their law clerks to prepare a memorandum on each case (a "bench memo") for the judge to review before hearing oral arguments. In some circuits, the law clerk for one judge may prepare a memorandum to be circulated among the three judges prior to oral argument. Most judges will study the briefs in advance of oral argument.

The appellant begins the argument. Because the judges have usually read the briefs and are therefore familiar with the issues, they sometimes begin questioning the attorney shortly after the argument begins. After the appellant's argument is completed, the appellee responds, followed by any reply by the appellant (if appellant reserved time for rebuttal).

Although the arguments are recorded so that the judges and their law clerks may later review them, some circuit judges require one of their law clerks to attend oral argument and take notes of important matters, citations of new authority, and concessions made during the argument.

Most cases are heard by a panel of three judges, but a case may be heard en banc in order to secure or maintain uniformity of decisions or in cases involving a question of exceptional importance. A case heard en banc is heard by all of the active judges on the court and any senior judge of the circuit who sat on the panel that originally heard the case (or, in the Ninth Circuit, by a "limited en banc," consisting of the Chief Judge and ten additional judges selected by lot).

En banc hearings are held only when ordered by a majority of the active judges on the court.

Some courts, such as the Second Circuit, hold hearings in only one location within the circuit, but most hold court in a number of locations.

G. Deliberation

After a case has been argued and submitted to the court, the panel of judges who heard the argument meets to arrive at a decision. In most courts, these meetings are held immediately after the completion of each day's arguments.

Appellate courts perform three distinct functions. First, they decide the controversies before them. Second, they supervise the courts within their jurisdiction. Third, they determine the growth and development of the common law and the interpretation of federal statutory and constitutional law within their jurisdiction. Each of these functions can become important during the decisional phase of an appeal because the court must not only reach the correct result but also explain in its opinion the rationale for its decision.

In most cases, the court arrives at a tentative decision at the first meeting. At that time, the presiding judge (the senior active circuit judge sitting on the panel) assigns the case to one member of the panel, who later writes an opinion to be submitted to the others for approval. When agreement is not reached so readily, panel members may exchange memoranda about the case and schedule additional meetings or telephone conferences for further discussion.

If a tentative agreement is not reached at the first conference, the law clerk may be called on to do any of the following: write a memorandum for the judge on particular issues or the entire case; review memoranda from other judges in order to discuss them with the judge; perform research; and perhaps write a draft opinion for consideration by the judge.

H. Opinion and Judgment

The final product of the court in most appeals is a written opinion setting forth the decision and the reasoning behind it. The increased number of cases and the burden of writing formal opinions in every case has caused appellate courts to use alternatives to formal opinions in many cases—such as cases involving only the application of settled principles to a specific fact situation. Several kinds of opinions, therefore, may be filed:

1. Authored

An opinion that reports the name of the judge who prepared it in addition to the names of the other members of the panel. Such an opinion is the conventional type reported in law school casebooks. It discusses the facts, the legal issues, the authorities, and the *ratio decidendi* (i.e., basis for the decision).

2. Per Curiam

Usually a short opinion dealing with a simple case involving issues that have been decided frequently. The opinion does not note the name of the judge who wrote it, but merely the names of the judges on the panel.

3. Dissenting

The opinion of one or more members of a panel disagreeing with the result reached by the majority.

4. Concurring

The opinion of one or more members of a panel, but less than a majority, agreeing with the result of the majority opinion, but disagreeing with the majority reasoning or choosing to make some other point.

5. Memorandum or Order

An opinion that is designed only to explain briefly to the parties why the panel decided the case the way it did. Such opinions are usually not published.

6. Summary

A mere statement that the district court judgment is affirmed or reversed.

Most circuits now have local rules or policies that guide the members of the court in deciding which cases deserve full opinions and which opinions should be published. Some circuits have rules prohibiting attorneys from citing unpublished opinions without first obtaining permission from the court.

When a panel has agreed on an opinion, it is initialed or signed by all three judges and forwarded to the clerk of court (or, in a few circuits, directly to the printer). In some courts, opinions to be published (and perhaps others) are circulated to all active judges on the court with a time limit for making suggestions.

I. Rehearing

The party who loses an appeal may file a petition for rehearing within fourteen days after judgment is entered. That petition attempts to persuade the panel that the decision was erroneous and should be withdrawn or revised. The prevailing party may not file a response to the petition unless one is requested by the court. Most petitions for rehearing are denied.

The losing party may also move for a rehearing en banc. That motion is circulated to all members of the original panel and all active judges who did not sit on the panel. Only the active circuit judges and any senior judge who was a member of the original panel may request a vote on the suggestion to rehear the appeal en banc; only the active circuit judges may vote on whether the appeal should be reheard en banc; and, if a rehearing en banc is granted, only active circuit judges and senior circuit judges from the circuit who were members of the original panel may sit on the rehearing. By local rule, a circuit may impose time limitations within which a member of the court may request an answer to a petition for rehearing or rehearing en banc or a vote on such a petition.

J. Mandate

The mandate is the document by which the court of appeals formally notifies the district court of its decision and by which jurisdiction for any necessary additional proceedings is conferred upon the district court. The mandate is issued by the clerk of court twenty-one days after judgment is entered unless a petition for rehearing has been filed or unless otherwise ordered by the court. If a petition for rehearing is filed, the mandate is issued seven days after denial of rehearing or, if a rehearing is granted, twenty-one days after the judgment is entered after rehearing. These times may be shortened or lengthened by court order. Fed. R. App. P. 41(a).

The losing party may request by motion that the issuance of the mandate be stayed in order to maintain the status quo during the pendency of an application for a writ of certiorari to the Supreme Court. The court of appeals may require that a bond be posted as a condition to staying the issuance of the mandate.

K. Motions

During the course of an appeal, the parties may file a variety of motions. Most of these are procedural and, to the extent permitted by the Federal Rules of Appellate Procedure, most courts have authorized their clerks of court to act on motions if they are uncontested. Common procedural motions that may be acted on by the clerk of court are motions for

- Extensions of time to perform any of the acts required by local rules or the Federal Rules of Appellate Procedure;

- Relief from specific requirements of the local rules or the Federal Rules of Appellate Procedure;

- Permission to alter the form or content of the record on appeal;

- Leave to file *amicus curiae* briefs;

- Delay in the issuance of the mandate; and

- Voluntary dismissal of the appeal.

Motions requiring action by a judge or panel of judges are those

- Relating to criminal cases or suits for post-conviction relief such as motions for

    - appointment of counsel;

    - leave to appeal in forma pauperis;

    - certificates of probable cause; and

– bail pending appeal;

- For stays or injunctions pending appeal;

- For leave to file interlocutory appeals;

- Relating to stays granted in the district court;

- For permission to file a brief containing more pages than the number fixed by the rules;

- Relating to the time to be allowed for oral argument; and

- To dismiss an appeal filed by the appellee.

In most courts, the staff counsel's office is responsible for processing these motions and otherwise assisting the court in disposing of them.

L. Emergency Proceedings

Both district courts and courts of appeals are frequently asked to make decisions on an emergency basis. In the appellate courts, these occasions usually arise when a litigant or a lower court is about to take some action that may cause irreparable injury. The potentially aggrieved party seeks redress by motion for stay or injunction pending appeal or by petition for writ of mandamus or prohibition. In the district courts, these matters usually arise through a request for a temporary restraining order.

Each court has developed internal procedures for handling these matters efficiently, but the procedures differ so much that it is not possible to make a generalized description. The law clerk and secretary must become familiar with the procedures established by the local rules and the judge's own practices.

M. Suggested Reference Material

Introducing the Federal Courts, Program 5: The Appellate Process (Federal Judicial Center, forthcoming August 1994) (one videocassette)

§ 3-5. Special Courts

The law clerk and secretary may also encounter litigation from one of the various special courts established by Congress. The name "special courts" derives from their specialized jurisdiction.

A. Court of Appeals for the Federal Circuit

The most important special court is the Court of Appeals for the Federal Circuit, created in 1982 by merging two existing courts, the U.S. Court of Customs and Patent Appeals and the appellate jurisdiction of the Court of Claims (the trial division of which is now the U.S. Court of Federal Claims, discussed in section 3-6.B *infra*). This court of appeals, based in Washington, D.C., has jurisdiction over appeals from the following: district courts in cases involving patents and certain claims against the United States; the U.S. Court of Federal Claims; the Court of International Trade; the Court of Veterans Appeals; the Merit Systems Protection Board; the patent and trademark office; the boards that decide government contract issues; and a few other Article I agencies.

B. Court of International Trade

The Court of International Trade, based in New York City, hears cases concerning the value or classification of imports. The judges of this court hold office during good behavior. Its judges may sit by designation on other Article III courts.

C. Special Courts with Revolving Membership

Congress has created some courts whose judges do not sit permanently on those courts but are assigned to them for terms of varying length in addition to their regular judicial assignment. These include:

1. Judicial Panel on Multidistrict Litigation

This panel was created to consider transferring civil actions involving one or more common questions of fact pending in different districts to a single district for coordinated or consolidated pretrial proceedings. The panel consists of seven judges (district and circuit) appointed by the Chief Justice. The panel maintains a roster of "transferee judges" to whom it assigns the cases it certifies for transfer. (For discussion of multidistrict litigation problems, see *supra* section 3-1.D.)

2. Special Court, Regional Rail Reorganization Act of 1973

It was created by Congress to resolve problems arising from the transfer of private railway property to the Conrail system. Its judges are chosen by the Judicial Panel on Multidistrict Litigation. 45 U.S.C. § 718.

3. Temporary Emergency Court of Appeals

This court has been abolished. It was created by Congress as part of the Economic Stabilization Act Amendments of 1970. Appeals formerly heard by the Temporary Emergency Court of Appeals are now heard in the U.S. Court of Appeals for the Federal Circuit.

§ 3-6. Article I Courts

Congress has created many tribunals to assist it in meeting its legislative responsibilities under Article I of the Constitution. These courts do not exercise judicial power conferred by Article III, and the judges are appointed for fixed terms rather than given lifetime tenure. They include the many administrative law judges serving in the executive agencies who hear disputes over claims and benefits, subject to review by agency officials.

A. U.S. Tax Court

The history of the U.S. Tax Court begins with the Revenue Act of 1924. The Act established the court as the U.S. Board of Tax Appeals in the executive branch of the government. In 1942, its name was changed to the Tax Court of the United States. As part of the Tax Reform Act of 1969, Congress reconstituted the Tax Court of the United States as the U.S. Tax Court.

The Tax Court has jurisdiction over controversies involving deficiencies determined by the Commissioner of Internal Revenue in income, estate, and gift taxes. The court also has jurisdiction to redetermine deficiencies in certain excise taxes and in windfall profits taxes; to redetermine liabilities of certain transferees and fiduciaries;

to issue declaratory judgments related to the qualified status of retirement plans, the tax-exempt status of charitable organizations, and the status of certain governmental obligations; and to decide certain cases involving the disclosure of tax information by the Commissioner of Internal Revenue.

The Tax Court uses the Federal Rules of Evidence and its own rules of practice and procedure. The Tax Court's decisions are generally reviewable by the courts of appeals and by the Supreme Court. In cases in which the amount of tax in dispute does not exceed $10,000, simplified procedures are available at the option of the taxpayer. In these cases, however, the decision of the Tax Court is final—it is not subject to review by any other court.

The Tax Court consists of nineteen judges appointed by the President, with the advice and consent of the Senate, to serve for terms of fifteen years. Its strength is augmented by Tax Court senior judges, who are recalled by the chief judge to perform further judicial duties, and by staff members who are designated special trial judges and are appointed by the chief judge.

The principal office of the Tax Court is located at 400 Second St., N.W., Washington, DC 20217. The court maintains a field office in Los Angeles, Cal., and conducts trial sessions in more than seventy-five other cities throughout the United States.

B. U.S. Court of Federal Claims

The U.S. Court of Federal Claims was originally called the U.S. Claims Court. It was established as an Article I court on October 1, 1982. The court has jurisdiction over claims brought against the U.S. government. The court is located in Washington, D.C. However, its jurisdiction is nationwide, enabling it to conduct trials in locations convenient to the parties involved in the case.

C. U.S. Court of Military Appeals

Congress established the U.S. Court of Military Appeals on May 5, 1951. The court is an appellate criminal court, hearing all cases involving military court-martials. It is located in Washington, D.C.

D. U.S. Court of Veterans Appeals

The U.S. Court of Veterans Appeals was created on November 18, 1988. It has exclusive jurisdiction to review the decisions of the Board of Veterans Appeals. The court's principal location is in Washington, D.C. It may, however, hold court anywhere in the United States.

Chapter 4. Court Governance and Administration

§ 4-1. Overview of Federal Judicial Administration

Each of the ninety-four district and thirteen federal courts of appeals is responsible for its own management. However, each is subject to statutory restrictions and policies set by national and regional judicial administrative agencies. The national agencies are the Judicial Conference of the United States and its agent, the Administrative Office of the U.S. Courts (AO). The Federal Judicial Center has educational and research responsibilities, and the U.S. Sentencing Commission has guideline-promulgating authority, but neither has administrative responsibilities for the federal courts. To the degree possible, administrative policy making is decentralized. Judicial councils in each regional circuit, with staff assistance by circuit executives, set administrative policy for the courts within the circuit, but the individual courts are responsible for most of the day-to-day administration. Clerks of the district courts (and district court executives in a few of the larger courts) and clerks of the bankruptcy courts provide staff assistance to their respective courts. Secretaries and, to a lesser extent, law clerks will at some time come into contact with most of these agencies.

§ 4-2. Chief Justice of the United States

The Chief Justice, who is presiding officer of the Supreme Court, presiding officer of the Judicial Conference of the United States, and chair of the Board of the Federal Judicial Center, often speaks for the federal judiciary on major matters in its relations with the other branches of government and with the public at large. The Chief Justice may appoint an administrative assistant to help with both internal Supreme Court administrative matters and matters related to the entire judiciary.

§ 4-3. Judicial Conference of the United States

At Chief Justice William Howard Taft's urging, Congress created the Conference of Senior Circuit Judges in 1922 to provide an annual forum in which the presiding judges of the courts of appeals could try to improve performance in the district courts by developing plans for intercircuit assignments and considering recommendations for case management improvements. In 1939, Congress transferred responsibility for federal court budget preparation, data gathering, and administrative support from the Justice Department to the newly created Administrative Office of the U.S. Courts, which Congress directed to function under the Conference's supervision. The Conference's name was changed in 1948, and district judges became members in 1957.

The Chief Justice presides over the Judicial Conference, which is composed of the chief judges of the courts of appeals, one district judge from each regional circuit, and the chief judge of the Court of International Trade. The circuit judges are Conference members as long as they are chief judges (presumptively seven years). The Chief Justice is directed by statute to call at least one annual meeting; the practice since 1949 has been to hold two meetings each year, one in the spring and one in the fall. Since 1987, the Executive Committee of the Conference has proposed the agendas for the meetings and acted on the Conference's behalf on limited matters between meetings.

The Conference is generally referred to as the federal courts' principal policy-making body for administration on the national level, but its organic statute (28 U.S.C. § 331) does not describe or suggest so broad a role. The statute directs the Conference to "make a comprehensive survey of the condition of business" in the federal courts, prepare plans for temporary assignment of judges, receive certificates of judicial unfitness from judicial councils, study the operation of federal procedural rules, and submit suggestions for legislation through the Chief Justice's report on Conference proceedings. Although Congress has vested relatively little authority directly in the Judicial Conference, the Conference has considerable practical authority, which arises from its statutory responsibility to supervise and direct the Administrative Office of the U.S. Courts, including the AO's control of the distribution of funds appropriated by Congress.

The committees of the Conference perform a vital role in the Conference's policy-making process. Normally, committees meet in person twice each year for one or two days to discuss and prepare materials for submission to the Conference prior to its next meeting; these meetings are supplemented by telephone conference calls, written memoranda, and occasional subcommittee meetings.

Almost all of the approximately 240 judges who serve on committees are life-tenured (district and circuit) judges rather than term-appointed (bankruptcy and magistrate) judges. In addition, some committees include Justice Department officials, state supreme court justices, law professors, and practicing lawyers. The Chief Justice makes committee appointments after receiving information from several sources, including applications from judges and advice from the Administrative Office.

§ 4-4. Circuit Judicial Councils and Circuit Executive

Congress created circuit judicial councils in 1939. The chief judge of the circuit is the presiding officer of each circuit judicial council. In addition to the chief circuit judge, each circuit judicial council consists of an equal number of circuit and district judges as determined by majority vote of active circuit and district judges of the circuit. 28 U.S.C. § 332(a)(1). Creation of the councils reflected a commitment to decentralized administration of the courts. The circuit judicial councils review numerous district court operational plans (for jury utilization and representation under the Criminal Justice Act, for example) and take action as appropriate. A council may also review final orders of the chief judge regarding complaints of judicial conduct if requested to do so by the person who filed the complaint or the judge complained against. Each circuit judicial council also reviews all local rules within its circuit to be certain they do not conflict with the national rules.

Each circuit judicial council has appointed a circuit executive and assigned that person duties specified in the statute. 28 U.S.C. § 332(e). The circuit executive's role is discussed at section 6-5 *infra*. The circuit council, by statute, meets at least twice a year.

§ 4-5. Chief Judges

Each court of appeals and each district court has a chief judge, as do bankruptcy courts with more than one judge. A vacancy in the chief judgeship of a court of appeals or district court is filled by the active judge who, at the time of the vacancy, is senior in commission, is under sixty-five years of age, has served on the court at least a year, and has not previously served as chief judge. A chief judge's term is limited to seven years. No judge may serve as chief judge beyond the age of seventy unless no younger judge is eligible to become chief judge or acting chief judge. Upon the chief judge's request, he or she may be relieved of the duties of that office and remain an active judge (see *infra* section 4-8). In that event, the active judge of the court next most senior in commission who meets the criteria and is willing to serve is designated by the Chief Justice as the chief judge. In bankruptcy courts with more than one judge, the district judges, by majority vote, designate one of the bankruptcy judges as chief judge. The chief district judge makes the designation if a majority of the district judges cannot agree.

Chief judges have no authority over the actual decision of cases by other judges. In judicial matters, their authority is exactly the same as that of any other judge.

A. Courts of Appeals

The chief judge for the court of appeals for any circuit is referred to as the chief judge of the circuit. He or she supervises the staff and most administrative matters for the court of appeals. Among numerous other responsibilities, the chief judge also does the following: presides at judicial council meetings and the circuit's judicial conferences; serves as one of the circuit's two representatives to the Judicial Conference; assigns circuit and district judges in the circuit to temporary duty on other courts in the circuit; certifies to the Chief

Justice the need for temporary assistance from additional judges from other circuits; and reviews complaints of judicial misconduct. In most circuits, the chief judge appoints committees of judges or individual judges to assist in various administrative matters.

B. District Courts

The chief judges of district courts have much of the responsibility for the administration of the court. Usually they supervise the clerk's office, the probation office, the pretrial services office (if there is one), and the administration of the magistrate judge system. They also exercise some oversight responsibility for the bankruptcy court. By statute, the chief judge is responsible for carrying out the rules and orders of the court that divide the court's business among the judges (28 U.S.C. § 137), and for appointing magistrate judges when a majority of the judges in the district do not concur (28 U.S.C. § 631(a)). In some district courts, the chief judge appoints committees of judges or individual judges to assist in various administrative matters. In some district courts, the judges meet regularly; in others, they consult each other only as the need arises. In most courts, the allotment of cases to judges is made randomly by the clerk of court, but the chief judge may, on occasion, make a special assignment for an unusual case, such as one of considerable length or complexity. The chief judge, however, has no jurisdiction over cases once they are assigned to another judge.

C. Bankruptcy Court

Chief bankruptcy judges have a more specific statutory mandate than circuit or district chief judges. Congress has directed chief bankruptcy judges to "ensure that the rules of the bankruptcy court and of the district court are observed and that the business of the bankruptcy court is handled effectively and expeditiously." 28 U.S.C. § 154(b).

§ 4-6. Circuit Judicial Conferences

The circuit, district, and bankruptcy judges of each circuit are required by statute to attend the annual or biennial circuit judicial conference to consider ways of improving the administration of justice in the circuit. 28 U.S.C. § 333. The statute mandates the court of appeals to prescribe rules for participation by the bar. The conferences vary considerably from circuit to circuit, but usually feature programs relating to problems in the administration of justice in the circuit.

§ 4-7. Federal Agencies of Judicial Administration

A. Administrative Office of the U.S. Courts

Congress established the Administrative Office (AO) in 1939 (28 U.S.C. §§ 604–612), at the request of the judiciary, to create an "administrative officer of the United States courts . . . under the supervision and direction" of the judicial branch rather than the executive branch. The director of the AO carries out the AO's statutory responsibilities and other duties under the supervision and direction of the Judicial Conference.

The AO's duties today extend well beyond those assigned in 1939, although the early duties are still basic: supervising administrative matters; gathering caseload statistics; procuring supplies and space; and preparing and administering the budget, with all the attendant financial management duties.

The AO's *Annual Report of the Director*, published along with the *Report of the Proceedings of the Judicial Conference of the United States*, provides detailed statistical data on all phases of federal court operations. The AO also publishes *The Third Branch*, a monthly newsletter for the federal courts that provides articles on legislation, Judicial Conference activities, judicial personnel changes, and other matters. In addition, it updates the *Guide to Judiciary Policies and Procedures*.

The Administrative Office Telephone Directory lists the AO's various offices and units.

B. Federal Judicial Center

In 1967, Congress created the Federal Judicial Center (FJC), at the request of the Judicial Conference, to consolidate research and continuing education programs for the federal courts in a single, independent agency. The Center and the Administrative Office maintain a close working relationship. The Center's policies are set by a board, chaired by the Chief Justice, that includes the Director of the Administrative Office as an ex officio member and six judges elected by the Judicial Conference. The Center is responsible for designing and sponsoring programs for the continuing education and training of judges and other court personnel, policy planning and research on matters of judicial administration, promoting study of the history of the federal courts, and assisting judges of state courts and foreign judicial systems in learning about the federal judiciary. It produces various publications and audiovisual materials available to judges and other judicial branch employees (some of which have been mentioned above). Current listings of available materials are found in the Center's *Catalog of Publications* and *Catalog of Audiovisual Media Programs*.

The organization of the Center is explained in its *Annual Report*; its key personnel are listed in the Administrative Office Telephone Directory.

C. United States Sentencing Commission

Congress created the U.S. Sentencing Commission in 1984 and directed it to establish federal sentencing policies and practices to guide judges in sentencing criminal offenders. 28 U.S.C. § 991. The Commission's seven voting members, appointed by the President, must include at least three federal judges. The Commission's initial guidelines went into effect on November 1, 1987, and apply to all offenses committed on or after that date. The Commission has the authority to submit annual guideline amendments to Congress, which automatically take effect 180 days after submission unless a law is enacted to the contrary.

§ 4-8. Active and Senior Judges

At the age of sixty-five, district and circuit judges may elect to become senior judges provided they meet the "rule of eighty"—that is, if the combined total of the judge's age and years of service equals or exceeds eighty. 28 U.S.C. § 371 (c). Taking senior status is at the discretion of the judge, who may continue to be an active judge until death. A judge who elects senior status creates a vacancy, which is filled in the usual manner by presidential appointment and senatorial confirmation. Judges on senior status have retired "from regular active service" (28 U.S.C. § 371(b)), but continue to receive the salary of an active judge on the same court if they are certified by the chief circuit judge as having met certain workload requirements. Senior judges who the circuit council certifies to be performing substantial judicial service are entitled to chambers and an office staff equivalent to that of active judges or to such lesser number of assistants as their work may require. Some circuits have adopted guidelines for staff requirements.

Senior judges often continue to serve their courts, usually taking a reduced caseload and requesting that they not be assigned certain types of cases, often classes of routine cases. Some senior district judges, for example, request that Social Security appeals or criminal cases not be assigned to them. Senior judges on appellate courts usually participate only in cases requiring oral argument. Particularly in recent years with the increasing caseloads in the federal courts, the services rendered by senior judges have been vital.

The Chief Justice may assign judges to serve temporarily in other circuits. Senior judges are sometimes especially appropriate choices for such assignments. The assignments may include protracted cases requiring an extended period of temporary service or high-profile criminal cases.

Judges who meet the "rule of eighty" may also "retire from the office," in which case they are no longer judicial officers. Retired judges may not continue to hear cases, but are entitled to an annuity equal to their salary at the time of retirement. 28 U.S.C. § 371(a). Of course, judges who do not meet the requirement of the "rule of eighty" may simply resign from office, thereby forfeiting all future pay and benefits.

§ 4-9. Budget Appropriations and Administration

The director of the Administrative Office, under supervision of the Judicial Conference, provides the Office of Management and Budget with the federal judiciary's annual requests for legislative appropriations to fund the various court operations for the forthcoming fiscal year. These are incorporated unchanged into the President's annual judiciary budget request, which is submitted to Congress, which in turn enacts a statute providing the courts with appropriations for the fiscal year.

Although the director of the AO has statutory responsibility for how the courts spend their appropriated funds, the AO has implemented an extensive program that delegates this spending responsibility to the courts themselves, under AO supervision. Clerks of court are responsible, under the chief judge's supervision, for receiving and disbursing funds and managing the budget. For example, the clerk of court disburses funds appropriated for travel and the court's normal operation and maintenance, and collects moneys received for court services and court-imposed fines, penalties, and forfeitures.

A. Suggested Reference Material

Russell R. Wheeler, Origins of the Elements of Federal Court Governance (Federal Judicial Center 1992)

Guide to Judiciary Policies and Procedures (Administrative Office of the U.S. Courts) (multivolume looseleaf; supplemented and updated irregularly)

Chapter 5. Chambers and Case Management

§ 5-1. Office Administration

Effective office management is essential to the prompt and efficient administration of justice. Discussed below is general information of which law clerks and secretaries should be aware to help chambers operate smoothly.

A. Security

The U.S. Marshals Service (discussed more fully at section 6-16 *infra*) is responsible for security of the court and its personnel. (Some courthouse security functions are delegated to the Federal Protective Service.) Law clerks and secretaries should become familiar with the marshals' court security plan in their courthouse. A judge may request a deputy from the Marshals Service to be present at certain times in the courtroom.

For security measures in connection with the mail, see *infra* section 5-1.D.

B. Keys

Law clerks and secretaries should obtain keys to the judge's office and the library. A key to the building will ordinarily not be needed because most federal courthouse buildings have one secured entrance through which all courthouse personnel must pass. After-hours or weekend entrance is usually gained by passing through security.

C. Telephone

Some judges instruct that the office telephone be attended during all working hours, including lunch periods. Many have installed an answering machine for use during lunch hours or when all members of the judge's staff are in the courtroom.

The telephone should be answered promptly. Identify the office (e.g., "Judge Smith's chambers"). Basic rules of politeness and etiquette apply. If the judge is not available to receive a call, offer to take the name, number, and message of the caller so the judge may return the call. Some lawyers hesitate to ask that a judge return their calls, but some judges prefer to do so, and the caller should be so informed. Other judges prefer to receive a detailed message so that a return call can be avoided; if so, callers should be encouraged to describe the reason for their call.

If the call relates to a case, the message should contain the name and number of the case. In addition, it should contain a description of the problem to which the call relates.

Do not keep a caller waiting on the line for any length of time. If a lawyer is put on hold while the law clerk determines the answer to the question, or while the lawyer waits to speak to the judge, someone should check back periodically to ask if the caller wants to continue holding.

Most judges prefer not to be interrupted in conference, and their calls should be held. Some judges also request that their calls be held at other times to allow them an uninterrupted period for concentrated activity. If the judge is not available, it is appropriate to say "The judge is in trial," or "The judge is in conference," or "The judge is out of the office," but some judges prefer that the reason for their unavailability not be communicated.

If the judge is not in the office, the appropriate response is, "The judge is not in the office at this time; may I take a message?" Some statements may convey a bad impression and should therefore be avoided (e.g., "The judge has said to hold all calls," "The judge can't be disturbed," or "The judge hasn't come in yet.").

Important phone calls may require documentation through correspondence or an office memorandum, and sometimes through a minute entry.

Official long-distance calls are to be made only on the Federal Telecommunications System (FTS), unless the judge specifically directs otherwise. The FTS consists of direct lines operated by the General Services Administration connected with the chambers of most federal judges, other government offices, and long-distance lines operated by access through the FTS. In 1992, the FTS network was converted from a seven-digit to a ten-digit network, allowing a court's commercial and FTS number to be the same. Long-distance calls by ordinary means result in additional billing by the telephone company directly to the judge's number. Such calls should not be placed unless the judge specifically so directs. Directory service is available only at an additional charge and should be used only when published telephone books do not contain the needed number. The judge's secretary will usually have instructions for telephone use.

Government telephones should not be used for personal calls except as specifically provided by regulations. Federal Information Resources Management Regulations stipulate:

> The use of Government telephone systems (including calls over commercial systems which will be paid for by the Government) shall be limited to the conduct of official business. Official business calls include emergency calls and calls considered to be in the best interest of the Government. A call may be considered in the best interest of the Government if it satisfies the following criteria:
>
> - It does not adversely affect the performance of official duties by the employee or the employee's organization.
>
> - It is of reasonable duration and frequency.
>
> - It could not reasonably be made at another time.

D. Correspondence and Other Mail

Most judges instruct a secretary or law clerk to open all mail except for envelopes marked "Personal" or "Confidential." Because federal judges are occasionally the targets of terrorists or disgruntled litigants, caution should be exercised when opening the mail. Common recognition points for letter and package bombs include

- foreign mail, air mail, and special delivery;

- restrictive markings (e.g., confidential, personal);

- excessive postage;

- handwritten or poorly typed addresses;

- incorrect titles;

- titles but no names;

- misspellings of common words;

- oily stains or discolorations;

- no return address;

- rigid envelope;

- lopsided or uneven envelope;

- protruding wires or tinfoil;

- excessive securing material such as masking tape or string; and

- drawings, diagrams, or illustrations.

If a letter or package arouses attention, do *not* attempt to open it. Instead, immediately notify the marshal's office or court security officer.

Incoming mail should be reviewed early in the day because it may relate to matters scheduled for that day. Much correspondence relates to cases pending before the court. Some will contain awaited memoranda of law on pending motions or trials. Some will ask for rescheduling or continuance of motion hearings or trials, though some judges require that such requests be made by formal motion. In the court of appeals, much of the correspondence will be from other judges and from the clerk's office.

Some mail will be library materials, such as new pocket parts to legal treatises. Most judges want to have specified advance sheets and other materials describing current decisions or legislation put on their desks for review before the materials are shelved in the library.

Depending on office procedure, either the judge, a secretary, or a law clerk will review correspondence and make an initial decision concerning how it should be handled. Correspondence that requires a response should be answered on the day it is received, if possible. In the trial courts, the judge may direct a law clerk or secretary to telephone all counsel with an oral response or to draft a letter to all counsel. When correspondence referring to a pending suit is forwarded to any counsel of record over the signature of the judge, law clerk, or secretary, copies should be sent to all other counsel of record, with the names of the other persons who are receiving copies (with the identifying abbreviation "cc") shown at the bottom of the letter. The issuance of identical communications to all parties signals that no ex parte communication has occurred and avoids consequent criticism. Letters requiring more complex responses (for example, a new date for the hearing of a motion) may require the judge's review.

Correspondence from an appellate judge will seldom be sent directly to counsel; it is sent to the clerk of court with instructions concerning how the clerk of court should reply, because the appellate judge writes for a panel or the court rather than individually.

Correspondence from the public (nonlawyers) is important because citizens have a right to courteous treatment. Also, the public's opinions about the fairness, responsiveness, and effectiveness of the judiciary are affected by the promptness and appropriateness of the court's answers.

In the district court, some of the correspondence from the public involves requests to be excused from jury duty. That subject is dealt with in section 5-3 *infra*. Some correspondence contains character references on behalf of a person convicted of a crime who is scheduled for sentencing. Judges differ in their handling of such correspondence. Most simply acknowledge receipt of the letter and refer it to the probation office.

Other correspondence from the public may express a reaction to a ruling of the court. Whether positive or negative, expressions of opinion by members of the public generally call only for courteous acknowledgment, not for an explanation or justification of the court's action. If a letter requests information about a ruling, most judges simply acknowledge receipt of the letter and send a copy of the opinion. If more information is requested, most judges refer the writer to the record. (See *supra* section 2-2.E.1 for comments regarding the relationship between chambers staff and the media.)

Some judges may wish to respond to a letter that indicates a misunderstanding concerning a significant fact, proceeding, or legal conclusion. Judges who adopt this policy may ask their law clerks to prepare a draft of a response for the judge to review. The response should not be argumentative or defensive; it should merely state the relevant facts or legal conclusion.

See *infra* section 7-2.G.3 for a discussion of correspondence from prisoners.

E. Opening Court

In most appellate courts, law clerks do not have the responsibility for opening court. In district courts, they frequently do. One common method is for the law clerk to rap on the door before the judge enters, open the door, then call out "All rise." The judge then enters and walks to the bench. The law clerk walks to the front of the bench and says: "The Honorable United States District Court for the ____ District of ____ is now in session." The judge usually stands during this call, then says "Please be seated," and sits.

F. Maintaining the Library

Each day's mail will bring something for the library: advance sheets, pocket parts, slip opinions, replacement volumes, and inserts for loose-leaf services. Filing these in their appropriate locations is usually the law clerk's responsibility, but may be done by the secretary. If the materials are put away daily, the chore of maintaining the library will not be burdensome. If the materials are left to accumulate, not only is the job more demanding but the library is incomplete and unreliable.

Every book received must be promptly rubber stamped to identify it as property of the United States. The law clerk or secretary should keep track of books borrowed by attorneys for courtroom use and should make sure that books are not taken outside the chambers and courtroom.

The law clerk should promptly reshelve books used during the course of research. They will then be easier to find, and the library will be neater. The law clerk or secretary should also be sure that legal pads, book markers, pencils, and pens are always available in the library.

G. Maintaining Office Records and Files

A law clerk or secretary may be assigned responsibility for maintaining some of the records in the judge's office, including the following:

- Case files;

- Trial schedules or calendars;

- "Tickler" records to remind the judge about future case activities;

- Indices to the judge's prior decisions;

- Indices to slip opinions; and

- Work papers relating to cases in progress.

Law clerks and secretaries may also find it helpful to make a collection of materials used frequently in the judge's office. This may include forms, office procedure checklists, and samples of work. These will be useful references and, if kept current, will be invaluable to successor law clerks and secretaries.

If case records are being used in the judge's chambers, either the law clerk or secretary should be certain that the records are not misplaced and are returned to the office of the clerk of court as soon as the judge or staff member has finished with them.

H. Preserving Chambers Papers for Historical Purposes

The chambers papers of a district or circuit court judge have historical significance as an essential supplement to the official court record. The following categories of papers in judges' chambers are widely considered valuable:

- All correspondence and background material concerning a case, including, but not limited to, memoranda between judges and law clerks and judges on an appeals panel, and drafts of orders and opinions. (Draft opinions that have handwritten comments on them, or that have been circulated to other judges and returned with their comments, should be retained.);

- Correspondence/memoranda concerning court administration;

- Correspondence/memoranda concerning activities on judicial committees;

- Communications between judges and members of the bar concerning legal activities in the community;

- Correspondence from the public on a case; and

- Correspondence with other prominent figures concerning issues of governance, politics, or law.

Secretaries and law clerks should keep in mind the following:

- When documents are created, they should include the date of creation and the name of the writer.

- The permanent record is, for the moment, still a paper record. All textual documents slated for preservation should be printed on paper. Repositories will not customarily accept computer disks as permanent records.

- If there is a question about whether a document belongs in the judge's chambers files or in the official case file, copies should be included in both places.

- Papers should be kept in clearly labeled folders in the original order that they were filed in chambers.

- Papers transferred to repositories should be sent in clearly labeled boxes designed for records transfer.

By long-standing custom, the chambers papers of federal judges are considered the personal property of the judge, to be preserved or disposed of according to his or her discretion. Therefore, judges who wish to have their papers preserved and made available as a historical resource after their tenure must make plans to deposit their papers with a repository. The most appropriate repository is one that has an established program for collecting manuscripts related to judicial or governmental programs and making them available to scholars.

If a judge makes an arrangement with a repository early in his or her career, chambers papers can often be transferred on an ongoing basis, clearing space in the judge's chambers while preserving valuable materials. Most judges have privacy concerns that most repositories are willing to accommodate; each agreement is drawn up individually between the repository and the donor. Papers transferred to a repository can be withheld from researchers until the judge decides research use is appropriate.

With the agreement of a repository, a judge may also make provision in a will for papers to be donated to the repository after the judge's death. If a judge dies without having made provision for the deposit or destruction of his or her papers, the decision for disposition is up to the judge's family or heirs. If the family wishes, the Federal Judicial History Office will assist in placing the papers.

The Federal Judicial History Office at the Federal Judicial Center will provide assistance to judges, secretaries, and court managers on all issues concerning judges' papers. Please call (202) 273-4180 with any questions.

I. Office Form Book

An office form book helps to educate new law clerks and secretaries and to provide continuity and consistency in office administration. The form book may contain samples of letters, orders, opinions, jury charges, minute entries, and office or file memoranda written by prior law clerks. The form book describes the format and method of presentation of written documents issued by the court or presented to the judge by the law clerk. These forms may be maintained on the computer either on hard disks or in the form of a macro (a function whereby several keystrokes can be carried out with one command).

J. Preparing for Out-of-Town Trips

Some federal judges must travel to other cities to attend court sessions, and most such judges require one or more law clerks and secretaries to travel with them. In addition, judges will often travel on court-related business. Arrangements for travel are usually made by secretaries. The following checklist may be handy when making such arrangements:

- If commercial transportation is to be used, make reservations as early as possible. Tickets are usually purchased with government charge cards. Government fares should always be used when available.

- Make necessary hotel or motel reservations (many hotels and motels give discounts to government employees).

- If necessary, a cash advance may be obtained by utilizing the ATM access functions of a government charge card (in the absence of a government charge card, cash advances may also be obtained using standard form 1038).

- If the judge is traveling to hold court in another location, prepare for the judge to take along

  - necessary case files and materials;

  - any personal notes or memoranda relating to the cases to be heard;

  - the judge's robe;

  - paper, pencils, stationery, and other needed supplies (if the site for the out-of-town session is one frequently used by the court, there may be a permanent stock of stationery and supplies);

  - necessary equipment such as a gavel, recording or dictating equipment, and a laptop or notebook computer and diskettes, if available;

  - the briefs and any other case materials; and

  - mailing labels and envelopes for returning material that the judge does not wish to carry back.

K. Travel Expenses

Judges, law clerks, and secretaries who travel on court business will be reimbursed for food, lodging, and related expenses according to the detailed rules set forth in *Guide to Judiciary Policies and Procedures*. These rules generally reimburse either a flat dollar amount per day, regardless of actual expenses, or itemized actual expenses not in excess of a fixed dollar amount. The judge's secretary should have forms for travel reimbursement.

L. Judge's Chambers Calendar

The secretary is usually in charge of maintaining the chambers calendar covering the judge's scheduled court proceedings and other activities. In appellate courts, the clerk of court advises the judge of panel assignments and hearing dates. The secretary will then schedule all other engagements and commitments, in consultation with the judge, around the hearings. In trial courts, the secretary usually confers with the judge and then typically advises the courtroom deputy in charge of scheduling as to the dates on which trials and hearings are to be set. The secretary will then schedule the judge's remaining commitments around the trials and hearings.

M. Supplies, Equipment, and Furniture

Generally, supplies, equipment, and furniture requests are given to the court's procurement officer, usually someone in the clerk of court's office.

N. Automation

The courts are increasingly assisted by computers. All chambers are equipped with personal computers for use by secretaries, and, in many chambers, law clerks also have access to personal computers. While these are used primarily for word processing, other computer assistance is available. CHASER (chamber access to electronic records), an automated case-management retrieval system for chambers that is now running in pilot courts, helps judges and chambers staff access docket sheets, calendars, and motions information, as well as various statistical and inventory reports and other data stored in the clerk of court's office. Some courts have PACER (public access to electronic records), which can now be made to perform many of the same functions. These systems enable the judge or staff to determine, among other things, pending cases and the date of most recent activity, all pending motions, all matters under submission, and compliance with pretrial orders and filing deadlines.

In many courts, law clerks have access (usually through the court library) to LEXIS and WESTLAW, computerized legal databases. Learning to use LEXIS and WESTLAW greatly increases a law clerk's ability to do efficient and thorough legal research.

Law clerks and secretaries should make a point of familiarizing themselves with the full range of computerized technology available in their courts. Training is available from sources within and without the judiciary. Staff should ask the court's automation support personnel or training specialist for information about training.

O. Extrajudicial Activities

Many judges engage in teaching, writing, lecturing, and other extrajudicial activities. While chambers staff may be called on to assist judges in these activities, the Code of Conduct for United States Judges prohibits judges from using staff for these purposes to any substantial degree.

§ 5-2. Local Court Rules and Administrative Policies

A. Local Rules

Federal Rule of Civil Procedure 83 and Federal Rule of Criminal Procedure 57 authorize district courts to adopt local rules. Federal Rule of Bankruptcy Procedure 9029 provides similar authority to bankruptcy courts. Local rules must be consistent with the national rules and may be abrogated by the circuit judicial council. 28 U.S.C. § 2077 directs the courts of appeals to publish their procedural rules, including internal operating procedures.

These local rules include the procedure for setting cases for trial, scheduling pretrial conferences, setting motions for oral argument, serving memoranda of law, and other details relating to trial. They may also state the procedure for admission of attorneys to practice in the specific district or circuit, the term of the court, the functions of the clerk of court, the rules regarding the filing of motions, and more specific data, such as the number of copies required to be filed, limitations on the length of memoranda, the time within which memoranda must be filed, and restrictions on page length, typeface, and margin size.

Each court of appeals has local rules concerning procedures for ordering transcripts, filing and docketing the appeal, calendaring, motions, summary disposition of appeals, setting cases for oral argument, time limitations on oral argument, petitions for rehearing, petitions for en banc consideration, and stay of mandate. The local rules and internal operating procedures (IOPs) of the circuits are printed in the *United States Code Annotated* following Title 28 of the Judicial Code.

Local rules of court and the court's internal operating procedures establish specific procedures in the district or circuit. A pamphlet copy of the district or circuit rules and internal operating procedures may be obtained at the office of the clerk of court. Immediately upon beginning work, law clerks and secretaries should obtain copies of these rules and procedures, carefully read them, and keep them available for ready reference.

Local rules are often revised by an order of the court. The law clerk or secretary should be certain to obtain all loose sheets and other addenda that have been adopted after the pamphlet was published.

B. Chambers Manual

Some judges have a chambers manual outlining how that judge expects his or her chambers to operate. Law clerks and secretaries should become familiar with such a manual if one exists.

§ 5-3. Case Management: The Trial Court

Most judges believe that the responsibility for moving a case through the trial court is not solely that of the attorneys, and the function of the court is not simply to be available if and when counsel want a hearing. The disposition of all cases as speedily and economically as is consistent with justice is of paramount importance. Private counsel have many personal reasons to delay proceedings: other clients, relative fees to be earned, procrastination, or lack of familiarity with procedures, to name but a few. Litigants whose cases are not promptly tried may conclude that the fault lies entirely with the courts. The Federal Rules of Civil Procedure are to be "construed to secure the just, speedy, and inexpensive determination of every action" (Fed. R. Civ. P. 1), and many judges consider this not only an instruction for interpreting the rules but a mandate to these goals. These judges believe that it is the duty of the courts to protect the public interest by participating actively in the process of moving cases from filing to determination. To carry out this duty, all courts have adopted civil justice expense and delay reduction plans under the Civil Justice Reform Act of 1990.

Effective docket control means that, early in the life of a case, the court should assume responsibility for guiding the case to a conclusion. A preliminary conference should be held, and dates for steps in the case fixed. This may include establishing deadlines for filing motions, a time limit for discovery, a date for counsel to take the next step in its prosecution, and preferably a trial date. For a succinct description of case management, consult the *Elements of Case Management* (Federal Judicial Center 1991). For specific techniques of case management, consult the *Manual for Litigation Management and Cost and Delay Reduction* (Federal Judicial Center 1992).

A. Office Status Sheets

Some judges maintain an office status sheet on a bulletin board in the chambers library or some other convenient location. Its purpose is to keep the judge, law clerks, and secretaries apprised of legal matters under advisement and awaiting disposition. When a matter has been taken under advisement, the secretary or law clerk assigned to the case should write it on the status sheet.

It is also a good practice for each law clerk to keep a personal status sheet, which can be revised each week. This sheet should list all of the matters for which the law clerk has responsibility, and it will enable the law clerk to make effective use of time and to remember all pending assignments. Some judges require weekly submission of personal status sheets.

Some judges require their secretaries to keep a list in their word processors of all pending matters, the initials or name of the law clerk assigned to work on the matter, and any other pertinent information. If such a list is maintained, the law clerk should be sure to keep the secretary advised of all matters assigned, matters completed, and other relevant status information.

Many judges use computers for docket control and to maintain case inventories and case-status records. While this is the most effective method, other systems may be employed provided they are regularly maintained and continually monitored.

B. Calendaring Systems

In multijudge trial courts, it is necessary to have a system for determining which judge is responsible for each case. In an individual calendar system, each case is assigned to a particular judge at the time it is filed, or soon thereafter, and that judge has complete responsibility for the case until it is terminated. All federal district courts now use this system and employ random case-assignment systems. There are also standard procedures for reassigning cases in which the original judge is disqualified, for assuring that related cases are all assigned to the same judge, and for special assignment of unusual and protracted cases. These are all described in the local rules.

C. Trial Scheduling and Preparation

A single trial may be set for a specific date, or the court may set multiple cases for trial on the same day. Some courts use the "trailing calendar" or "trailing docket," in which the court schedules a number of cases for trial beginning on a stated date. The cases are tried in the order reflected by the schedule. Counsel themselves are responsible for obtaining information from the court and from the attorneys whose cases precede them on the calendar about the progress of those cases, so that they may be ready to go to trial whenever the court reaches their case.

More than 90% of all civil cases filed are disposed of before trial by rulings on motions or by settlement. Many judges and commentators believe that the highest quality of justice results from a freely negotiated settlement arrived at between equally skilled and prepared advocates. Settlement achieves a solution to a controversy earlier and at less cost than a trial. When the case involves only the interests of the parties, negotiated settlement may be desirable. If the case involves an issue of public importance, however, adjudication may be the method of disposition that better meets the needs of justice. Some judges, therefore, may not press for settlement of such cases. Whatever settlement negotiations may occur, the lawyers should be thoroughly prepared to try a case if and when the case is reached. Some courts issue specific written instructions to attorneys stating their responsibilities for trial preparation.

If settlement is to be reached, negotiations should be timely completed. Last-minute settlements may disrupt the court's schedule, leaving the judges, and sometimes jurors, with unscheduled time. Counsel have spent time preparing for trial, witnesses have been subpoenaed, and the litigation costs have increased.

The trailing calendar and other multiple-case-setting devices alleviate some problems caused by last-minute settlement by providing substitute cases to replace those that do not go to trial. Although this relieves the court's problems, it does not reduce the problems caused to litigants and counsel by eve-of-trial settlements.

D. Jury Management

1. Random Juror Selection

The selection of grand and petit jurors is governed by 28 U.S.C. §§ 1861–1878. Each district has a jury selection plan that has been approved by the circuit judicial council and the chief judge or the chief judge's designee.

The goal of the selection process is to assure "grand and petit juries selected at random from a fair cross section of the community in the district or division wherein the court convenes" (28 U.S.C. § 1861), and to avoid excluding any citizen "from service as a grand or petit juror . . . on account of race, color, religion, sex, national origin, or economic status" (28 U.S.C. § 1862).

The process of selecting prospective jurors is managed by the clerk of the court or, in a few courts, by a jury commission consisting of the clerk and one citizen resident within the district, as determined in each court's jury selection plan. The process is carried out under the supervision and control of the court.

Although jury selection processes may differ slightly in each district, the process is generally as follows:

- A random selection of prospective jurors' names is made by computer or manually, using voter registration lists or other sources specified by the court's plan. The names thus selected are placed in a master "jury wheel," which today is usually a computer file. The minimum number of names in the master jury wheel must be one-half of 1% of the number on the source lists, or 1,000, whichever is less;

- As needed by the court, names are drawn publicly at random from the master jury wheel, and jury-qualification questionnaires are sent to those persons whose names are drawn;

- From the responses to the questionnaires, a determination is made as to which persons are qualified for jury service and which persons are disqualified, exempt, or excused;

- The names of those determined to be qualified are placed in a second jury wheel consisting of qualified jurors;

- As needed, names are selected from the qualified jury wheel, and lists of the names selected are prepared; and

- Summonses are issued to the necessary number of persons needed for the jury venire several weeks in advance of each trial calendar advising those summoned of the time and place to report for jury service.

2. Exemptions, Disqualifications, and Excuses

A person is deemed qualified for jury service unless the person is

- Not a citizen of the United States;

- Unable to read, write, and understand English with a degree of proficiency sufficient to satisfactorily complete the juror qualification form;

- Incapable of rendering satisfactory service because of mental or physical infirmity; or

- Charged with (or has been convicted in a state or federal court of record of) a crime punishable by imprisonment for more than one year without subsequent restoration of civil rights. 28 U.S.C. § 1865.

Some district courts have adopted other grounds for exemptions. These are based on public interest and are specified in the court's jury selection plan. 18 U.S.C. § 1863 requires the plan to provide for the exemption of members of the armed forces in active service; members of the fire or police departments of any state; and public officers of the federal, state, and local governments who are actively engaged in the performance of official duties.

Jury service is a citizen's duty as well as a privilege, and excuses are not readily granted. A person may, however, be excused from jury service temporarily if the court finds that such service would result in undue hardship or extreme inconvenience. In such a case, the name of an excused juror is placed back in the qualified jury wheel. If approached about an excuse, the law clerk or secretary should not express any opinion regarding the request but should simply agree to transmit it to the judge for action or inform the individual of the judge's procedure for handling such requests.

The court and all its staff should make every effort to see that those called for jury selection are treated with courtesy.

In multiple-judge courthouses it is common for several judges to begin jury trials at different hours to obtain maximum use of people summoned for jury duty, sending persons examined and not selected to another courtroom so they can be examined for selection on another jury, and sometimes using jurors who have served in one trial in a succeeding trial.

When prospective jury panels report for possible selection in a case, they should be segregated from other people in the courtroom. A portion of the spectator section should be cleared for their exclusive use.

3. Juror Orientation

Most courts conduct an orientation program for new jurors to inform them of their responsibilities and to explain the trial process. Two orientation videos are available in most courts, one for grand jurors, the other for petit jurors.

4. Voir Dire

In most courts, the judge conducts voir dire examination of jurors. Federal Rule of Civil Procedure 47 and Federal Rule of Criminal Procedure 24, however, authorize the judge to permit the lawyers to conduct voir dire. If the judge conducts the voir dire, the rules authorize counsel to submit specific questions or areas of inquiry that they want the judge to probe. In some courts, magistrate judges conduct voir dire. Most circuits permit this in civil cases, though some require consent of the parties. The Supreme Court has held that a magistrate judge may conduct voir dire in a criminal case if the defendant consents (Peretz v. United States, 111 S. Ct. 2661 (1991)), but not if the defendant objects (Gomez v. United States, 490 U.S. 858 (1989)).

Jurors are usually free to go where they wish during recesses, and they may go home at night. Occasionally, however, when there is unusual publicity about the trial or reason to believe that someone will attempt to exert improper influence on jurors, the court may direct that the jury be sequestered. When this occurs, the jury is kept together at all times and is supervised by deputy marshals when court is not in session. Jurors in criminal and civil cases are sometimes sequestered from the time they begin deliberating until they reach a verdict.

5. Jury Supervision

In most courts, a deputy marshal is responsible for jury supervision. However, this responsibility may be assigned to a law clerk. When such assignment is made, the law clerk should be present in the chambers early enough in the morning to accommodate those members of the jury who arrive before the normal court time. The jury room should be open and available for use by the jurors as they arrive.

If it is the judge's policy to permit the jury to take notes, either the deputy clerk or the law clerk should, before the trial begins, place pads and pencils in numbered manila envelopes for distribution to the individual jurors. Extra pads, pencils, and envelopes should also be placed in the jury room for use during deliberations.

Law clerks responsible for jury supervision must ensure that there is no improper communication between jurors and litigants, lawyers, witnesses, or others attending court—whether in the courtroom, jury room, or hallways adjacent to the courtroom and chambers.

The law clerk may also be required to steward the jury during deliberations. Some courts require the law clerk to take a special oath with respect to this duty just before the jury retires. Once the oath is taken, the law clerk assumes primary responsibility for guarding the jury until relieved of this duty by the judge. The law clerk must remain outside the jury-room door during the entire deliberation process and must take every reasonable precaution to ensure that the jurors do not come into contact with other people, especially the litigants, their attorneys, or any witnesses. The law clerk must *never* comment on the evidence, the litigants, the attorneys, or the witnesses to any juror (or, for that matter, to anyone else). If a juror has any questions about the trial, at any stage, the law clerk should simply state that such questions should be addressed to the court in writing. The law clerk must not answer the question, however simple it may appear.

E. Distributing Opinions

Federal Rule of Civil Procedure 52(a) requires the judge to make findings of fact and conclusions of law in all actions tried without a jury or with only an advisory jury. The rule permits the judge to do this orally on the record or in writing in an opinion or memorandum. The district judge may also wish to write a formal opinion to explain rulings on particular motions. The judge's secretary sends the original of the findings or the opinion and the original of any order for judgment to the docket clerk for filing in the official record. Then the secretary or clerk of court sends a copy of each set of findings or the opinion to each counsel of record, making and distributing other copies in accordance with the judge's instructions. In most district courts, the clerk of court handles the distribution of opinions, but in a few district courts, this responsibility falls to the law clerk or secretary.

The judge decides whether the opinion or findings are to be published. Publication connotes inclusion not only in a traditional case reporter, but also in on-line computer services, such as West Publishing Company's WESTLAW and Mead Data Central's LEXIS, and in specialized reporting services. The publication procedure in district courts is not uniform. Some opinions may be sent only to West Publishing Company and Mead Data; others (of unusual importance) may be sent to the Bureau of National Affairs; some may be sent to specialized publishers, such as American Maritime Cases. Unless someone else is given this task, the law clerk or secretary should check with the judge to determine whether the judge wishes the opinion to be published and should make such distribution as the judge directs. In each case, the opinion should be accompanied by a cover letter from the judge; the judge may have a form letter for this purpose.

§ 5-4. Special Duties of Law Clerks and Secretaries to Bankruptcy Judges

The duties of a law clerk and secretary to a bankruptcy judge are generally similar to the duties of those working for district court judges. Of course, the subject matter of bankruptcy courts is limited to civil proceedings and most trials are bench trials.

Because the volume of cases and proceedings in bankruptcy court is generally greater than in other trial courts, law clerks and secretaries must be especially organized and efficient. (Of course, effective time management is critical to all law clerks and secretaries; there is almost always more work than can readily be done.) Bankruptcy hearings are generally more numerous and expedited than those in district court. For the chambers staff, that means more scheduling problems, more substantial prehearing preparation of memoranda, and shorter time limits. It also means more pressure from attorneys telephoning to ask about procedures, for expedited schedules, about the disposition of motions, and various other questions. Like district court judges, bankruptcy judges differ in their attitudes about direct contact between chambers staff and attorneys.

Some bankruptcy judges hold court in more than one place. Law clerks and secretaries to those judges usually have substantial duties in preparing for travel, including assembly of materials (such as appropriate portions of case records necessary for the trip). The law clerk will usually have extra duties in the additional places of holding court because the other staff available may not be as complete as in the home court.

The organization of the bankruptcy courts is discussed at section 3-3.A *supra*.

§ 5-5. U.S. Magistrate Judges

Before 1968, U.S. commissioners were responsible for issuing federal arrest and search warrants, holding preliminary hearings, and trying petty offenses with the consent of the defendant. In 1968, Congress abolished this office and assigned the duties performed by commissioners to a new class of judicial officers, United States magistrates. 28 U.S.C. §§ 631–639. In 1990, Congress changed the title from magistrate to magistrate judge. The authority of magistrate judges now derives primarily from the Federal Magistrates Act of 1968 (28 U.S.C. §§ 631–639), as interpreted by *Mathews v. Weber* (423 U.S. 261 (1976)), and as amended several times since. The Magistrates Act permits each district court to appoint full- and part-time magistrate judges in such numbers and locations as may be determined by the Judicial Conference of the United States.

The duties of a magistrate judge include, but are not limited to, the following:

- Administering oaths on criminal complaints and affidavits in support of search warrants;

- Issuing arrest warrants or summonses upon a finding of probable cause in a criminal complaint;

- Issuing search warrants upon a finding of probable cause from the affidavit in support of the application;

- Conducting preliminary hearings in criminal cases to determine whether there is probable cause to believe that an offense has been committed and that the defendant has committed it;

- Conducting pretrial detention hearings pursuant to 18 U.S.C. § 3141–3145; and

- Revoking or modifying probation or supervised release if such restrictions were previously imposed by a magistrate judge.

In addition, to the extent authorized by the appointing court, a magistrate judge may, pursuant to 28 U.S.C. § 636:

- Try persons accused of, and sentence persons convicted of, misdemeanors when specifically designated to do so by the district court (28 U.S.C. § 636(a)(3), 18 U.S.C. § 3401), unless the defendant elects to be tried before a district judge. A federal misdemeanor is an offense for which the maximum penalty is no more than one year's imprisonment. See also the *Rules of Procedure for the Trial of Minor Offenses Before United States Magistrates* (promulgated by the Supreme Court on June 1, 1980, and reprinted as part of the one-volume edition of Title 18 prepared by West Publishing Co. and available in each judge's chambers);

- Serve as special master in civil actions and in proceedings pursuant to 28 U.S.C. §§ 2254 and 2255 when designated to do so by the district court;

- Assist a district judge in the conduct of civil and criminal pretrial or discovery proceedings;

- Perform a preliminary review of applications for post-conviction relief and make recommendations to facilitate the decision of the district judge to whom an application has been assigned; and

- Serve as a judge for the trial of civil cases if all parties consent.

For additional matters that may be referenced to magistrate judges, see *Bench Book* at sections 1.27 and 2.09, and *Legal Manual for United States Magistrate Judges,* Chapter 3, Jurisdiction of United States Magistrate Judges (Administrative Office of the U.S. Courts June 1991).

The local rules of court for each district describe the assignments that may be made to magistrate judges. In some courts, magistrate judges are used to the full extent permitted by the statute. For example, many judges delegate pretrial management of all civil cases to magistrate judges; others refer matters on a case-by-case basis. The law clerk for a district judge should examine the local rules of court and ascertain the practice of the court in this regard.

A district's full-time magistrate judges are appointed for a term of eight years by a majority of the judges of the district. Part-time magistrate judges are appointed for a term of four years. A magistrate judge may be removed from office by a majority of the judges of the district for incompetence, misconduct, neglect of duty, or physical or mental disability.

To qualify for appointment as a magistrate judge, a person must be under seventy years of age, a member of the bar in good standing of the area to be served, competent to perform the duties of the office, and unrelated by blood or marriage to any judge of the appointing court. Some district courts impose additional requirements, such as a minimum number of years in law practice.

§ 5-6. Case Management: The Appellate Court

Each appellate court has a system for assigning cases, managing motions, and scheduling hearings. Because appellate courts do not take evidence or use jurors, the processes are simpler than in trial courts.

Federal appellate courts are required by statute to publish their internal operating procedures, and law clerks and secretaries should consult local procedures.

A. Motions

The processing of motions on appeal is described in the appellate court's internal operating procedures. Federal Rule of Appellate Procedure 27 describes the prescribed form for motions. Some motions are decided by the clerk of court, some by a single judge, and some by a panel of judges. The local rules list those motions on which a single judge or the clerk of court has authority to act. Circuits differ on whether oral argument is heard on motions. In some circuits, there is no procedure for oral argument of a motion, unless specially requested by the court, and in other circuits, substantive motions, such as those for bail, stays, injunctions, dismissal, or remand, are heard weekly as a matter of course.

B. Screening

Federal Rule of Appellate Procedure 34(a) provides that oral argument shall be allowed in all cases unless, pursuant to local rule, a panel of three judges, after examination of the briefs and record, unanimously decides that oral argument is not needed. Oral argument is to be allowed "unless (1) the appeal is frivolous; or (2) the dispositive issue or set of issues has been recently authoritatively decided; or (3) the facts and legal arguments are adequately presented in the briefs and record and the decisional process would not be significantly aided by oral argument." Fed. R. App. P. 34. Pursuant to this rule, most circuits employ a procedure known as "screening" to select those appeals to be decided without oral argument (i.e., on the briefs and written record alone). When the last brief is filed, the appeal is sent to a judge (or staff attorney) for screening classification. The policy in various circuits differs. For example, the Eleventh Circuit Court of Appeals requires that, for oral argument to be denied, all three judges of a screening panel must concur on three matters: that oral argument is not required; the result; and the full text of the opinion, without separate concurrences. If all three criteria are met, the appeal is decided without oral argument. See the Eleventh Circuit's Local Rule 34-3.

The screening process may also lead the court to conclude that the appeal is of special importance and warrants more than the time usually allowed for oral argument. The panel may then set it for an extended oral argument and notify counsel that additional time has been allowed.

Other methods are used to expedite the court's caseload. In response to the large number of appeals filed, in 1974 the Second Circuit adopted a Civil Appeals Management Plan (CAMP) providing for a program of preargument conferences pursuant to Federal Rule of Appellate Procedure 33. The purpose of the CAMP procedure is to encourage parties in civil cases to reach voluntary settlements early in the appellate process and, in those that do not settle, to improve the quality of briefs and arguments and resolve procedural problems. The preargument conference is conducted by the staff counsel. A number of the circuits have adopted some form of preargument conference procedure, although the procedures differ considerably in purpose and method.

See generally Judith A. McKenna, Structural and Other Alternatives for the Federal Courts of Appeals 37–53 (Federal Judicial

Center 1993) for a description of various alternative methods of processing appellate cases.

C. Order of Assignment of Appeals for Oral Argument: Calendar Preparation

Once an appeal is assigned to a panel, all motions are acted upon by that panel rather than by a separate motions panel.

In most courts of appeals, one person (usually the clerk of court) selects the appeals to be heard during a particular session of court without knowing which judges will be sitting. At the same time, someone else (usually the chief judge or a committee of judges) assigns the judges who will sit at that session without knowing which appeals will be heard. Thus the workloads are equalized, but no person can influence the assignment of an appeal to a particular judge or panel of judges.

Courts that sit in more than one location try to schedule an appeal for hearing at the location most convenient to counsel. In the Tenth Circuit, for example, an appeal in which all counsel have offices in Oklahoma will be scheduled for hearing in Oklahoma City unless that scheduling would create undue delay in its disposition.

When scheduling appeals for a particular session, the person making the assignments operates under guidelines established by the court as to the number and kinds of appeals to be scheduled for each day. Some courts make an effort to equalize the workload for each day of the session and, if more than one panel is sitting, to equalize the workload among the panels. Others try only to equalize the workload for a week of sitting. In some circuits, the person making the assignments also schedules appeals with related issues or facts for the same panel. Alternatively, if a controlling appeal is awaiting decision by another panel in the court, the hearing may be delayed until the controlling appeal is decided. In most circuits, the fact that the Supreme Court has granted certiorari in an appeal presenting the same issue is not considered sufficient reason to postpone assignment, although the panel may, after hearing argument, decide to await the Supreme Court's decision before preparing an opinion.

The senior active judge on the panel is the panel's presiding judge. During the course of a hearing, the court is under the control of the presiding judge. The crier, under the supervision of the judge, opens and closes court and maintains order and decorum. Each judge's law clerk or the crier has responsibility for supplying the courtroom with paper, pencils, drinking water, and other materials needed by the judge and counsel.

Each court has its own rules and customs regarding protocol, dress, and courtroom behavior.

Courts of appeals do not have reporters, although they tape-record oral argument for the use of the court. Litigants who wish to have transcripts must request court approval and arrange for a reporter or some other person to prepare the transcript. Many courts maintain lists of qualified persons for this purpose.

D. Order of Opinion Writing

Although there is no statutory requirement that opinions be issued within a fixed time or in any particular order, most judges determine priority based on three criteria: the importance and urgency of the decision; the nature of the appeal, giving direct criminal appeals priority over civil cases; and the order in which appeals were argued to the court (or in which briefing was completed).

At any time, each judge will have drafts of opinions in various stages of preparation. The length of time between preparation of the initial draft and issuance of the final opinion varies greatly depending upon the number and complexity of issues that must be treated, the extent of suggested revisions and additions by other members of the appellate panel, and whether concurring or dissenting opinions are also issued.

The internal operating procedures of most courts include rules concerning the maximum time period before a proposed opinion should be submitted to other members of the panel by the writing judge and the time within which those panel members should respond. Law clerks and secretaries should become familiar with these rules.

E. Distributing Opinions

After an opinion is issued, the original is filed with the clerk of court. When the opinion is filed, the clerk of court prepares a judgment in accordance with the operative language of the opinion. Fed. R. App. P. 36. The judgment is usually quite simple, merely stating whether the judgment of the trial court is affirmed, reversed, or otherwise modified, and giving directions on remand.

In most appellate courts, the clerk of court arranges for reproduction or printing of the opinion and distributes the copies. In some circuits, the law clerk or secretary sends an opinion to a printer who then distributes the copies, called "slip opinions." Reproduction is usually accomplished through private contract printers, but may be done in-house by members of the clerk of court's office staff. If a printer is used, it usually provides galley proofs of the slip opinion, which are proofread by the authoring judge's secretary or law clerks. The slip opinions of several circuits are reproduced by West Publishing Company. In those circuits for which it is not the official printer, West prepares its copy for publication in the *Federal Reporter 3d* and sends galley proofs to the authoring judge. The judge's secretary or law clerks proofread the galleys, make any necessary changes, and return them to West for publication. These steps are eliminated in the circuits for which West is the slip opinion publisher. In those circuits, editorial changes are made on the slip opinion.

The law clerk, secretary, or clerk of court distributes copies of the final slip opinion to the parties, to all judges in the circuit, to traditional and computer on-line publishers, and to a large number of subscribers including government agencies, law offices, and law schools. In those circuits in which West is the official printer, it mails these copies.

Chapter 6. Relations with Other Court and Justice System Personnel

Law clerks and secretaries work closely with other court personnel. Familiarity with the other personnel and what they do will help chambers staff run a smooth office.

§ 6-1. The Clerk of Court

The clerk of a United States district court is appointed by and serves at the pleasure of the court. Except in the handful of courts that have a district court executive (see *infra* section 6-2), the clerk of court serves as the chief operating officer, implementing the court's policies and reporting to the chief district judge. The clerk's responsibilities include the following:

- Recruiting, hiring, classifying, training, and managing the staff of the clerk's office;

- Developing and implementing a records management system to properly maintain and safeguard the official records of the court;

- Developing and maintaining a system to ensure the proper collection, accounting, and disbursement of funds and securities in the court's custody;

- Developing budgetary estimates of future staffing requirements and other substantive expense items, such as supplies, equipment, furniture, services, and travel;

- Collecting and analyzing statistical data that reflect the performance of the court;

- Managing the jury selection process, including the responsibility for making a continuing evaluation of juror utilization;

- Maintaining liaison with all branches of the court and related government agencies;

- Preparing and disseminating reports, bulletins, and other official information concerning the work of the court; and

- Coordinating the construction of court facilities and periodically inspecting such facilities.

§ 6-2. District Court Executives

District court executives serve on four of the largest federal district courts (E.D.N.Y., S.D.N.Y., N.D. Ga., and S.D. Fla.), and the Eastern District of Michigan has a "court administrator." In those courts, the executive performs the overall management responsibilities that would otherwise be assigned to the clerk of court, and the clerk's duties are related primarily to the management and monitoring of the cases filed with the court.

§ 6-3. The Courtroom Deputy and the Docket (Minute) Clerk

Courtroom deputies' duties and responsibilities vary significantly from court to court. The deputy, sometimes called a "minute law clerk" or "case manager," is an employee of the clerk of court's office, although the deputy serves the judge to whom the deputy is assigned and may have a desk in chambers.

Nearly all courtroom deputies record the minutes of the court and assist the judge with scheduling trials or hearings on motions. The deputy must keep the judge aware of all calendar activity. The deputy handles communication with the attorneys and schedules their appearances for hearings.

Other duties of courtroom deputies include the following:

- Administering oaths to jurors, witnesses, and interpreters;

- Maintaining custody of trial exhibits;

- Entering or causing to be entered on the permanent records of the clerk's office a description of all relevant actions taken in open court or in chambers (usually called a minute entry);

- Serving as liaison between the judge's chambers and the clerk of court's office; and

- Performing routine clerk's office duties as needed and when available.

The docket clerk (sometimes called the "case systems administrator") works in the office of the clerk of court and is responsible for maintaining the official records for each case pending before the judge. The docket clerk also makes the docket entries, recording all filings in a case with the clerk of court. Anyone who wants to review the docket must obtain access from the docket clerk. In most courts, these dockets are now automated. Except by order of the court or the clerk, a record may be taken from the clerk of court's office only by the judge. Some docket clerks assemble the records of cases to be heard at a motion hearing or at trial. Usually, the docket clerk is responsible for knowing where the record is at all times.

§ 6-4. The Appellate Clerk's Office

Each court of appeals has a clerk who is appointed by and serves at the pleasure of the court. The clerk of court appoints necessary deputies and clerical assistants with the approval of the court. The number of authorized employees and their salary schedules are established by the Administrative Office.

The primary duties and responsibilities of a court of appeals clerk are as follows:

- Maintaining the files and records of the court;

- Ensuring that all papers filed comply with the Federal Rules of Appellate Procedure and the rules of the court;

- Entering all orders and judgments of the court;

- Scheduling cases for hearing under guidelines established by law, rules, and orders of the court;

- Distributing needed case materials to the members of the court;

- Collecting, disbursing, and accounting for required fees;

- Arranging for reproduction and distribution of the court's opinions;

- Giving procedural assistance to attorneys and litigants;

- Maintaining the roster of attorneys admitted to practice before the court;

- Administering oaths;

- Providing clerical staff for courtroom services; and

- Providing necessary statistical case information to the court and the Administrative Office.

In addition, the court may authorize the clerk of court to act on certain kinds of uncontested procedural motions.

§ 6-5. The Circuit Executive

Each circuit's judicial council appoints a circuit executive. Although specific duties of circuit executives vary considerably from circuit to circuit, often they include a full range of administrative tasks, some of which are performed in the court of appeals while others are circuit-wide. Tasks in the courts of appeals may include administering nonjudicial matters, especially the personnel system and budget. Circuit-wide tasks may include conducting studies and preparing reports on the work of the courts; serving as the circuit's liaison to state courts, bar groups, the media, and the public; and arranging circuit judicial council and conference meetings. The circuit executive may also maintain an accounting system or establish a property control and space-management system. Some circuit executives provide advice and assistance on automation and circuit-wide training; others assist judges and committees in delicate areas such as processing judicial complaints.

§ 6-6. The Crier

Each court of appeals has authority to employ criers, who also serve as bailiffs and messengers. The crier attends sessions of court and announces openings of court, recesses, and adjournments. As bailiff, this employee maintains order in the courtroom under the direction of the presiding judge. The crier also provides messenger services as needed by members of the court.

In some courts, as a money-saving measure, law clerks serve as bailiffs. In these circuits, the presiding judge of each panel or a person in the clerk of court's office arranges for this duty to be rotated among the law clerks for the three panel members.

§ 6-7. Other Law Clerks and Secretaries

While it is important for law clerks and secretaries to know the roles of and establish sound professional relations with various personnel in the judicial system, it is especially important for them to know the roles of the other members of the chambers staff and to enjoy a healthy working relationship with them.

Most judges have all of their law clerks perform the same functions. Some judges have one permanent law clerk as well as another with a one- or two-year commitment. The permanent law clerk, already thoroughly familiar with the judge's practices and office administration, may play a more significant role than the rotating law clerk. Most district judges, however, no longer have permanent law clerks.

Each judge has a system for assigning work to law clerks, and each makes an effort to balance the workload. In order to equalize the work among the law clerks, allocations may be made on the basis of how much work will be required on a particular case. If a law clerk has a preference for a particular subject matter, a judge may try to accommodate that preference.

Although there are sometimes salary differences between law clerks (e.g., one law clerk is in the second year of clerking and the other is in the first), the responsibilities are usually the same. In district courts, the law clerks may, during alternate weeks, exchange the primary responsibility for administrative matters such as opening court, assembling files and records for the motion day, or preparing the conference room for a pretrial conference. Such assignments are flexible, and each law clerk should be cooperative in assisting the others when there is more work than can readily be completed in the time available.

In chambers with more than one secretary, assignment of tasks among the secretaries differs from court to court. In some courts, one secretary occupies a senior position and delegates duties, while in other courts, the secretaries agree among themselves on the division of labor. Likewise, in some courts, secretaries share responsibility for all chambers' operations, while in other courts, individual tasks are divided. Regardless of the approach decided on, a good working relationship and open communication among the secretaries will help chambers operate smoothly.

§ 6-8. Pro Se Law Clerks and Staff Attorneys

District courts with heavy prisoner filings may appoint pro se law clerks to review civil cases filed by prisoners, including petitions for writ of habeas corpus and complaints for violations of civil rights under 42 U.S.C. § 1983. Pro se clerks assist the court by screening the complaints and petitions for substance, analyzing their merits, and preparing recommendations and orders for judicial action, including orders of dismissal.

Each circuit has a staff attorneys' office employing as many lawyers as the circuit has active appellate judges. The administrative manager of the office is usually called the director of the staff attorneys' office or the senior staff attorney. One or more of the other staff members may also be assigned supervisory duties.

Although the precise duties assigned to the staff attorneys' office vary from circuit to circuit, the following tasks are generally assigned:

- Reviewing correspondence from litigants (usually pro se) in order to determine whether any communications are legally sufficient to constitute an appeal or a request for mandamus. Many of the letters or purported pleadings are prepared by a prisoner without legal assistance and consist of incomplete handwritten papers that are difficult to read and understand. When deciphered, they may be sufficient to constitute an appeal or petition for writ. If the correspondence, however, does not present an issue that may be considered by the court, the staff attorney may be authorized to so advise the author. If the correspondence is sufficient to invoke the court's jurisdiction, the staff attorney is usually directed to prepare a memorandum stating the issues in the case and, after doing any necessary research, to brief the issues.

- Reviewing appeals and applications for mandamus involving collateral attacks on state or federal criminal convictions. The staff attorneys' office usually reviews each such petition, analyzes the legal issues, prepares a memorandum of law concerning each issue raised, and recommends the disposition of the case. In some instances, the district court may have denied the certificate of probable cause that is the prerequisite for an appeal in forma pauperis, or may have failed to act on a request for such a certificate. If so, the staff attorney makes a recommendation concerning whether such a certificate should be issued. In many instances, the case will be sent to a panel of the court for decision on the merits without oral argument. In others, when the appellant is proceeding pro se, the staff attorney may recommend to the panel of judges to whom the case will be assigned that counsel be appointed. A panel of the court, however, makes the final decision in each case.

- Preparing memoranda of law concerning the issues in, and recommended disposition of, motions.

- Preparing memoranda of law concerning the issues in, and recommended disposition of, some criminal and civil cases. Because of the volume of work, most courts assign this duty to staff attorneys only in those types of cases most likely to involve repetitive presentation of similar issues or relatively easier issues. All others are assigned directly to a panel of judges.

- In most circuits, assisting in case management and in settlement procedures. The Second Circuit, for example, has a Civil Appeals Management Program directed by two staff attorneys.

- In some circuits, dividing cases into various categories, based on their expected difficulty, so as to assist the person who assigns cases to panels in allocating the anticipated workload equitably.

- Other duties assigned by the court.

The staff attorneys' office may work under the supervision of the chief judge, a committee of judges, a single judge, a senior attorney, the circuit executive, or the clerk of court. Some staff attorneys are employed for terms of one or two years in duration; others serve for longer periods. Judges frequently call the law clerks who work in their chambers on their personal staff "elbow law clerks." Staff attorneys are professionals entitled to the same respect.

§ 6-9. Court-Appointed Experts

Federal Rule of Evidence 706 authorizes the court to appoint expert witnesses. Such witnesses may be particularly helpful to the court and the jury when the experts who testify for the opposing sides render such diametrically opposite views that they appear to be advocates rather than impartial witnesses. The compensation of court-appointed expert witnesses is taxed against the parties in civil actions in the proportion the court directs. In criminal cases and civil cases involving just compensation under the Fifth Amendment, the expert's compensation may be paid with government funds.

For more information, see Joe S. Cecil and Thomas E. Willging, Court-Appointed Experts: Defining the Role of Experts Appointed Under Federal Rule of Evidence 706 (Federal Judicial Center 1993).

§ 6-10. Special Masters

Federal Rule of Civil Procedure 53 authorizes any district judge before whom an action is pending to appoint a special master. A special master is an impartial expert designated to hear or consider evidence or to make an examination with respect to some issue in a pending action, and to make a report to the court. A special master may be appointed in either a jury or a nonjury matter.

A referral to a special master may be expensive and time-consuming. Rule 53 states that such referral "shall be the exception and not the rule." Litigants are entitled to a trial of every issue unless an "exceptional condition" is shown. Yet when issues in a jury case are so complicated that the jurors are incapable of dealing with them unaided, the court may enlist the aid of a master to make findings on specific issues. In a jury case, these findings are admissible as "evidence of the matters found." The special master may be called to testify in the case, and, if called, is subject to cross-examination, like any other expert. The court may also appoint a special master to assist the court in bench trials when the complexity of the case so requires or to work with the parties and counsel in attempting to settle complex cases.

Any person who has particular competence to consider a complex matter may be appointed; thus a master may be, for example, a certified public accountant, an appraiser, or an economist. A special master's compensation is determined by the court and taxed as costs.

Magistrate judges may serve as special masters when appointed by the court pursuant to rule of court (28 U.S.C. § 636). Their services as special masters are particularly helpful because they are officers of the court with experience in fact-finding and judicial procedures, and their appointment does not add to the expense of litigation because they are not paid additional compensation.

§ 6-11. The Court Reporter

Each district court has permanent court reporters in numbers approved by the Judicial Conference. The standard ratio is one reporter per active judge. Judicial Conference policy requires court reporters to work for the court (in a pooling arrangement) rather than for individual judges, although the implementation of this arrangement varies with the number of judges and the places of holding court in the district. In practice, in some courts individual court reporters work primarily in the courtroom of a specific judge. However, a court reporter must adhere to the court's plan for pooling reporters and is not assigned to work only for a specific judge.

The duties of the court reporter include the following:

- Recording all court proceedings verbatim by shorthand or by mechanical means;

- Transcribing all arraignments, pleas, and proceedings in connection with the imposition of sentence in criminal cases, or filing a voice or sound recording of the proceedings (28 U.S.C. § 753); and

- Transcribing any proceedings upon request of a judge or any party to a proceeding.

Court reporters are federal court employees subject to the supervision of the court, but they also collect personal fees for transcripts prepared for parties at rates determined by the court and the Judicial Conference. Transcripts are usually prepared only after a trial is completed and an appeal filed. Litigants may, however, request daily transcripts by notice in advance. If they do so, the reporter arranges for assistance from other reporters, because each can take and transcribe only a few hours of the proceeding in that limited time. The reporters charge extra for this service, which is paid for by the litigants. That charge too is regulated by the court, subject to maximum limits set by the Judicial Conference. Because they earn private income, court reporters must provide their own equipment and supplies and may not use government postage for their correspondence.

The reporter must file a copy of every transcript with the clerk of court. This is a public record that may be inspected by any person without charge during the business hours of the clerk's office.

Subject to Judicial Conference regulations, district judges and bankruptcy judges may direct the record to be taken by electronic sound recording rather than by a court reporter. If the court does so, an employee of the clerk of court is responsible for operating the equipment and seeing to the preparation of any requested transcripts. Statutes and rules govern the process of recording specific proceedings before magistrate judges. Electronic sound recording is used more extensively by magistrate and bankruptcy judges than by district judges.

§ 6-12. The Librarian

Each court of appeals maintains a library at its headquarters, and those circuits with jurisdiction over a large geographic area have additional branch libraries at other locations. These libraries are primarily for the use of the judges and their staffs, but are generally open to members of the bar, employees of other governmental agencies, and the public.

Each library is managed by a librarian appointed by and serving at the pleasure of the court. The librarian may be responsible to the chief circuit judge, a committee of judges, the circuit executive, or the clerk of court, as determined by the court.

In addition to the usual responsibilities involved in managing a library, some librarians publish a periodic newsletter describing new publications and acquisitions and listing books and articles of particular interest to their court. They may also make recommendations for new acquisitions to the library or, in some circuits, act on the recommendations of the judge responsible for the library.

Each circuit library has one or more staff members who have special training in legal research and can help law clerks and judges in research. In some circuits, for example, the library staff will prepare a legislative history of a statute for a judge upon request.

Law clerks whose chambers are near circuit libraries will find it advantageous to use them frequently: They have many more volumes than the judge's smaller working library. The circuit library also has facilities for computerized legal research, including WESTLAW and LEXIS, and for general research on NEXIS. If the judge is not in a city that has a main or branch library with such facilities, a staff member at the main library may be willing, upon request, to undertake computer research and furnish the results by telephone or mail. Most librarians will mail books to a judge or a law clerk working in another city or will photocopy materials needed for research. They will also try to borrow from other libraries materials that are not available in their own.

The Law Library of the Library of Congress offers limited photocopying and research assistance to federal judges. The Law Library can compile indexes to federal legislative histories. Computerized databases of current legislative materials, including the *Congressional Record,* are available, as are rare treatises and extensive collections of American and foreign law periodicals. The Law Library can also perform bibliographic searches on specific subjects, though the personnel are not in a position to do extensive research. To request materials, a law clerk or a judge should write to or call the Chief of the American–British Law Division of the Law Library, Library of Congress, Washington, DC 20540, (202) 707-5077.

§ 6-13. The Probation and Pretrial Services Offices

Each district court appoints probation officers, including a chief probation officer. Probation offices with more than thirty officers also have a deputy chief probation officer. Some probation offices—for example, those with many probationers with drug-related or organized-crime convictions—establish supervisory units.

Probation officers serve at the pleasure of the court. Their salaries are set by the director of the Administrative Office under the supervision and direction of the Judicial Conference.

The responsibilities and duties of a probation officer include the following:

- Conducting presentence investigations and preparing presentence reports on convicted defendants;

- Supervising probationers and persons on supervised release;

- Overseeing payment of fines and restitution by convicted defendants;

- Supervising persons transferred under the Victim and Witness Protection Act; and

- Completing investigations, evaluations, and reports to the Parole Commission (in non-guidelines cases) when parole is being considered for an offender or when an offender allegedly violates parole.

The 1982 Pretrial Services Act directed that pretrial services be provided in all federal judicial districts. The services include evaluating persons proposed for pretrial release, monitoring and assisting those released, and reporting to the court on these activities (see 18 U.S.C. § 3154). Some district courts (especially small districts) provide pretrial services through their probation office; others have separate pretrial offices. The circuit council must approve creation of a separate office.

The chief pretrial services officer is selected by a panel composed of the chief circuit judges, chief district judges, and a magistrate judge, or their designees. The chief pretrial services officer appoints other officers with the court's approval.

§ 6-14. Public Defenders

The Criminal Justice Act of 1964 requires each district to have a plan to ensure that federal defendants are not deprived of legal representation because they cannot afford it. 18 U.S.C. § 3006A. In some districts, this need is met entirely by assigning cases to private attorneys who are paid under the Criminal Justice Act. Districts in which at least 200 appointments are made annually, however, may establish either public defender organizations or community defender organizations.

Federal public defender organizations are staffed by attorneys who are federal employees; the court of appeals appoints the federal public defender, who appoints assistant federal defenders. Community defender organizations are nonprofit defense-counsel-service groups authorized by the plan (which is required by the Act) to provide representation. Although federal public defender office attorneys and staff are federal employees paid by funds administered by the Administrative Office, they are not part of the district court staff. Their location in the judicial branch is primarily for the purpose of administrative convenience.

§ 6-15. United States Attorneys

In all cases in which the United States is a party, a representative of the Department of Justice is the attorney for the government. The representative is usually the U.S. attorney or an assistant U.S. attorney for the district in which the case is pending, but in some cases the representative will be a special assistant from the Department of Justice. In some situations, such as federal tax refund suits against the United States, a lawyer from the Department of Justice may have primary responsibility for defense of the case, and the U.S. attorney may serve as co-counsel of record. When the government party is a federal agency, such as the Equal Employment Opportunity Commission, agency counsel will usually represent the government party.

Each judicial district has a U.S. attorney, appointed by the President with the advice and consent of the Senate. The U.S. attorney is appointed for a term of four years, but is subject to removal by the President. If a vacancy exists in the office, the Attorney General may appoint a U.S. attorney, but that person may not serve for more than 120 days from the date of appointment. If the vacancy remains, the district court for the district in which the vacancy exists may appoint a U.S. attorney to serve until the President fills the vacancy. 28 U.S.C. § 546. Assistants to the U.S. attorney are appointed by, and may be removed by, the Attorney General.

The authority of a U.S. attorney is set forth in 28 U.S.C. § 547. The responsibilities generally include the following:

- Prosecuting all criminal offenses against the United States;

- Prosecuting or defending for the government all civil actions in which the United States is a party;

- Defending collectors or other officers of the revenue or customs in actions brought against them for official acts; and

- Prosecuting proceedings for the collection of fines, penalties, and forfeitures owed to the United States.

In connection with prosecutorial duties, the U.S. attorney (or an assistant U.S. attorney) is usually present during sessions of a federal grand jury but may not remain while the grand jury is deliberating or voting.

§ 6-16. United States Marshals Service

The President, with the advice and consent of the Senate, appoints for each judicial district a U.S. marshal who serves for a term of four years, but who, like the U.S. attorney, is subject to removal. The marshal, in turn, appoints deputies.

The U.S. Marshals Service is part of the Department of Justice and is responsible for moving prisoners, supervising the department's Witness Security Program, apprehending federal fugitives, executing all writs, process, and orders issued by the courts, and, of most direct interest to chambers' staff, providing security to the court and its personnel.

The marshal develops a court security plan, subject to review and approval by each district court's security committee, providing basic security services to judges and supporting personnel in that district. Under some plans, judges have emergency buzzer buttons beneath their desks and beneath their benches in the courtroom; if the button is pressed, an alarm sounds in the marshal's office. The marshal also has a deputy present in court whenever the judge so requests. Marshals and their deputies are authorized to carry firearms and may make arrests without a warrant within statutory and constitutional limits. Marshals and their deputies may exercise the same powers as sheriffs of the state in which they are located.

Although the parties themselves are ordinarily responsible for the service of process and subpoenas in civil cases, Federal Rule of Civil Procedure 4(c)(2)(B) provides that a summons and complaint shall, at the request of the party, be served by the marshal on behalf of a person authorized to proceed in forma pauperis, on behalf of the United States or an officer or agency of the United States, or by order of the court in special cases.

In many places, the marshal or the marshal's deputy is in complete charge of the jury. Law clerks are sometimes told to avoid all contact with the jurors. The law clerk should inquire about and become familiar with the special procedures in the court. See also *supra* section 5-3.D.5 on jury supervision.

§ 6-17. The Federal Bureau of Prisons

The Federal Bureau of Prisons manages the penal and correctional institutions maintained by the United States. Its director is appointed by the Attorney General.

When the judge sentences a person convicted of a federal crime, the order of commitment merely consigns the defendant to the custody of the Attorney General. Although the judge may recommend a preferred place of imprisonment, the Attorney General has the final authority to designate the actual place of confinement.

The bureau must provide suitable quarters, care, subsistence, and safekeeping for all persons held under the authority of the United States; provide for the protection, instruction, and discipline of all persons charged with or convicted of offenses against the United States; and provide technical assistance to state and local correctional institutions and officials. Each judge has a pamphlet describing all institutions maintained by the Bureau of Prisons, their facilities, and their programs.

In most judicial districts, there is no federal jail for the confinement of persons awaiting trial or after sentencing, so federal prisoners are confined in a state institution, under a contractual arrangement.

A judge may permit a sentenced defendant to report directly to the place of confinement. This avoids interim detention in state institutions that may be crowded or otherwise undesirable, and it saves the government the expense of transportation. If the prisoner is dangerous, is likely to escape, is unreliable, is not likely to report on time, or cannot afford transportation, the judge is likely to require the marshal to maintain custody of the prisoner and to transport the prisoner to the institution designated by the bureau.

For further information on the individual federal prisons, refer to *Federal Correctional Facilities,* an annual booklet available from the Office of Public Affairs, Federal Bureau of Prisons, U.S. Department of Justice.

§ 6-18. Federal Law Enforcement Agencies

Apart from the U.S. attorney's office, the U.S. Marshals Service, and the Bureau of Prisons, there are other federal law enforcement agencies that law clerks and secretaries may come in contact with during criminal trials. A brief description of them follows.

- *Federal Bureau of Investigation (FBI)*—investigates violations of certain federal statutes, collects evidence in which the United States is or may be an interested party, and performs other duties imposed by law or presidential directive, such as performing background checks on judicial nominees. The FBI is a bureau of the Department of Justice.

- *Drug Enforcement Agency (DEA)*—is the primary narcotics enforcement agency for the United States. It is a bureau of the Department of Justice.

- *Immigration and Naturalization Service (INS)*—administers the Immigration and Nationality Act; tries to prevent unlawful entry, employment, and receipt of benefits by those not entitled to them; and apprehends or removes those aliens who enter or remain in the United States illegally or whose stay is not in the public interest. The INS is a bureau of the Department of Justice.

- *International Criminal Police Organization–United States National Central Bureau (INTERPOL–USNCB)*—facilitates international law enforcement cooperation as the U.S. representative to INTERPOL, an intergovernmental organization of over 150 country members. INTERPOL–USNCB is a bureau of the Department of Justice.

- *Bureau of Alcohol, Tobacco, and Firearms (ATF)*—enforces and administers firearms and explosives laws as well as those laws covering the production, use, and distribution of alcohol and tobacco products. The ATF is a bureau of the Treasury Department.

- *Internal Revenue Service (IRS)*—administers and enforces federal internal revenue laws and related statutes, except those relating to alcohol, tobacco, firearms, and explosives. The IRS is a bureau of the Treasury Department.

- *United States Customs Service (USCS)*—collects the revenue from imports and enforces customs and related laws. The USCS is a bureau of the Treasury Department.

- *United States Secret Service*—not only provides security to high government officials, but enforces federal laws relating to currency, coins, and obligations or securities of the United States or a foreign government. The Secret Service is a bureau of the Treasury Department.

§ 6-19. State Courts

In most instances, a case that is brought in federal court may also be brought in state court. Although some cases *must* be brought in federal court, many more must be brought in state court. Each state has its own court system, and not all state court systems are alike. Some federal courts have established working relationships with state and local courts to help resolve scheduling conflicts, to share some services (such as jury rolls), and to promote cooperation in addressing common problems.

State–federal judicial councils facilitate good relations between the federal and state courts. Such councils are usually created by orders of the state supreme court and the federal district court or court of appeals. Activity of state–federal judicial councils has varied over the years and across the country. Some councils that lapsed into inactivity have been rejuvenated by vigorous chief district judges or chief circuit judges. Council agendas frequently include procedures to improve handling of federal habeas corpus petitions, reduce scheduling problems when attorneys are due in federal and state court simultaneously, and treat other potential sources of friction or opportunities for cooperation between the two systems.

Chapter 7. Legal Research and Writing

§ 7-1. Research

No judge has time to review all of the authorities bearing on each legal principle at issue in a case. Legal research is, therefore, the most important task of any law clerk. While it is rare that a judge will ask a secretary to do legal research, a secretary may be asked to help with editing, citation checking, and preparing routine orders carrying out the judgment rendered in the judge's opinion. Although this chapter is primarily targeted to law clerks, secretaries may find useful information here.

A well-crafted judicial decision can be made only in the context of precedent; the law clerk's role is to make sure the judge has the material with which to understand the jurisprudence related to the case. This cannot be accomplished by relying on the lawyers' briefs and research, however eminent the lawyers may be. Adequate judicial research includes not only checking the authorities cited in the briefs to determine their relevance and the accuracy of the citations, but also conducting independent research to determine whether the lawyers have overlooked controlling precedent or any helpful authority that may not be precedential.

The following suggestions may be of assistance:

- Understand the *purpose* of the research project. For example, the extent and depth of research for a bench memo is less than that for an opinion.

- Understand the *facts*. Judges apply law to specific factual situations, and if the facts of prior cases are distinguishable, those decisions may have little relevance, even if the same legal principle is at issue.

- Understand the *legal issue*. It helps to restate the issue in writing; articulation helps to clarify the issue and often indicates whether the researcher's understanding is adequate and precise.

If the legal area in which the issue arises is unfamiliar, perform a preliminary survey of the field utilizing secondary sources such as

- specialized treatises and texts (e.g., the Federal Judicial Center's series of monographs);

- casebooks;

- law review articles;

- loose-leaf services;

- ALR annotations (these can be particularly helpful; some experienced researchers include ALR as an early step in any research project); and

- legal encyclopedias.

Verify all secondary-source statements of the law. It is sometimes difficult to distinguish the author's opinions from the decisions cited.

- Identify useful West *key numbers* pertinent to the subject through

  - cases cited in the parties' briefs;

  - cases or key numbers located through the preliminary survey of secondary sources referred to above; and

  - examination of the appropriate key number outlines of the West Digest System.

- Examine the *headnotes* under the identified key numbers in the *Modern Federal Practice Digest* or other appropriate digests to locate cases on point.

- Use *computerized research*. If WESTLAW or LEXIS is available, search for additional authorities. Plan your search carefully in advance, however, to avoid wasting computer time.

- In cases involving federal statutes, examine the annotations to the appropriate statutes in *United States Code Annotated*. In cases involving state statutes, refer to the annotations in the state-statute source.

- *Read the opinions in full.* Carefully examine the actual opinions to determine their applicability to the problem.

- Distinguish the *holding* of the case from dicta.

- Read all *dissents* and *concurrences.* These special opinions may be particularly helpful in understanding complex or novel legal questions.

- Find *binding precedent.* Distinguish carefully between controlling and persuasive precedents. A state court decision on a procedural matter is usually not binding on a federal court, but a substantive decision of a state court may be controlling in a diversity case.

  Check to find whether there is conflicting authority within the circuit.

- *Shepardize, cite check,* or "auto-cite" (LEXIS or WESTLAW) any cases found to be on point to locate or determine

  - their continued authority;

  - more recent decisions;

  - similar cases from a controlling jurisdiction; and

  - more authoritative or better reasoned decisions.

- *Exhaust all sources.* If you have not located appropriate precedents, turn to secondary sources, or Shepardize or cite check similar but noncontrolling cases or analogous cases with the hope of locating more controlling precedents, or ones at least more similar to the one to be decided. Be sure to look up cases *cited* within your primary case; often, the cases on which an opinion relies are more on point than the primary opinion itself.

- *Use legal indices.* It is frequently helpful to consult the *Index to Legal Periodicals* and the *Current Law Index* for

  - case notes on key decisions (these are listed separately by case name); and

  - articles on critical problems.

- Do not overlook the American Law Institute's *Restatements of the Law,* both in final and draft form, and the model and uniform codes. (The Uniform Acts can be found in Martindale–Hubbell.)

- Consult the *librarian* if you need help. The librarian can be of great assistance, particularly in obtaining legislative histories, less frequently used reference works, and materials from other libraries.

- Use the *judge's files.* If the judge maintains an indexed file of his or her prior opinions (as many do), consult these files. They may be extremely helpful if they contain work on a case similar to the one being researched.

The law clerk usually relays the results of his or her research to the judge in writing, by either a memo or a draft opinion. However, judges will sometimes want an oral briefing, particularly when the information is needed quickly.

A. Current Advance Sheet and Slip Sheet Reading

In addition to research on specific cases, law clerks have a professional responsibility to keep up with developments in the law. Read all Supreme Court opinions as promptly as possible. Most courts receive these opinions first in *United States Law Week* and shortly thereafter in Supreme Court slip sheets. Both appellate and district court law clerks must read all slip opinions issued by their circuit as soon as possible: They are mandatory precedent to district courts and law of the circuit for other panels of the circuit court. The law clerk should immediately call to the judge's attention any opinion bearing on a pending case. District court law clerks should also review all opinions of their district that appear in the advance sheets of the *Federal Supplement.*

If time permits, law clerks should review decisions published in the *Federal Reporter* and *Federal Rules Decisions.* Because of the large number of opinions now being published, it may not be possible to read the full text of all opinions. After reviewing the headnote of each case, the law clerk should read in full at least those opinions applicable to cases pending before the judge or presenting issues frequently occurring in the court, as well as other decisions of particular interest.

§ 7-2. Writing

A. General Rules

Some judges do all of their own writing, while relying on their law clerks only to prepare internal research memoranda—others expect their law clerks to draft opinions and orders in final form, suitable for filing (with the judge's approval). Some judges assume personal responsibility for writing final opinions in cases that have been tried, but require their law clerks to prepare drafts of opinions disposing of preliminary motions. Regardless of the drafting process, decision making remains exclusively the judge's responsibility.

A law clerk may be assigned writing tasks for some or all of these kinds of documents:

- Memoranda to the judge;

- Orders and minute entries (in the district court); orders and short per curiams or other brief dispositions (in the courts of appeals);

- Opinions including findings of fact and conclusions of law (in the district court); both memorandum orders and opinions (in the courts of appeals); and

- Correspondence.

Law clerks must write clearly, concisely, and logically. Certain general rules of good writing style are as follows:

- *Prepare an outline before starting.* The best way to organize your thoughts and ensure that everything pertinent is included is to prepare a logical sentence or topical outline before beginning to write. Such an outline is essential before writing a draft opinion or any long document.

- *Introduce the subject.* At the outset, let the reader know the subject of the document. When preparing a memorandum on a specific issue, begin with a precise statement of the issue, followed by your conclusions as to its resolution. If preparing an

opinion or a memorandum summarizing an entire case, identify the parties, explain at the outset the history of the case,
and state the issues, their resolution, and the action taken by
the court (e.g., judgment vacated, motion for summary judgment denied, affirmed). While it is critical to state the relevant
and material facts, do not include inconsequential information
that does not bear directly on the question to be decided.

- *Avoid the use of generic terms as specific identifiers.* Federal Rule of
  Appellate Procedure 28(d) states:

  > Counsel will be expected in their briefs and oral arguments
  > to keep to a minimum references to parties by such designa-
  > tions as "appellant" and "appellee." It promotes clarity to use
  > the designations used in the lower court or in the agency
  > proceedings, or the actual names of parties, or descriptive
  > terms such as "the employee," "the injured persons," "the
  > taxpayer," "the ship," "the stevedore," etc.

  The same policy applies in district courts.

- *Follow the proper format.* The judge may require a special organization and arrangement of intraoffice written materials and
  may have standardized formats for other written materials.
  Learn these standard formats and follow them. (Examples from
  past cases can be found in the judge's files.) The judge's secretary can also advise you whether the judge has a prescribed
  format.

- *Be accurate and give appropriate references.* Be careful to quote accurately from a cited authority. Be certain that cited authority
  has not been overruled or qualified. Some judges require their
  law clerks to give citations to the sources of factual statements.
  Thus, if a particular fact is established by Smith's deposition, its
  statement is followed with "(Smith dep. p. 10)." This reference
  allows the judge to locate the statement easily, read it in context, and verify its accuracy. Often, lawyers will support their
  statements of fact in a brief by citing a deposition, a transcript
  of trial, or an exhibit. You should verify those citations before
  incorporating them.

- *Write succinctly, clearly, and precisely.* Good legal writing is simple, brief, and clear. Unnecessarily abstract or complex words and phrases, flowery language, or literary devices may interfere with the reader's ability to understand the point. Unless the judge instructs otherwise, leave embellishment to the judge.

- *Subdivide.* In a lengthy opinion or order, the reader may find it easier to follow if the material is divided into subparts, each labeled with letters, numbers, or short subtitles.

B. Editing

The four primary goals of editing are

- to correct errors in grammar and punctuation;

- to eliminate ambiguities and promote clarity;

- to improve the manner and order of presentation of the law or facts; and

- to improve the writing style.

Editing includes deleting words and phrases that may create confusion, eliminating redundant material, and correcting verbosity. Similar principles apply whether you are editing your own work or that of another law clerk or the judge.

- If you are editing your own work, you should set the draft aside and work on something else for a while before beginning editing. A fresh view may suggest improvements that might not otherwise occur to you.

- Read the material to be edited aloud; this may disclose previously unnoticed problems.

- Ask a co-clerk to read and comment on the draft, especially if he or she has not worked on it.

- Brevity and clarity are both important. Short, simple sentences are generally better than lengthy, compound, or complex sentences. However, strings of sentences of the same length are monotonous. A series of short sentences should be broken with an occasional longer one.

- The use of excessive punctuation may indicate that the sentence should be broken into two or more sentences.

C. Style

Each judge has a different writing style. Some prefer simple declarative sentences and use plain language. Others employ complex sentences and a varied vocabulary. Some use metaphor and simile to make a point. Whatever the judge's personal style, most judges prefer that their law clerks try to write in the manner that the judge has adopted. The judge issues opinions year after year; continuity in style is desirable. Read several of the judge's prior opinions to become familiar with his or her style. If in doubt, ask the judge what stylistic embellishment he or she desires.

An increasing number of judges avoid using masculine pronouns when speaking generally or hypothetically, using non-gender-specific language instead (e.g., "he or she" or "the defendant" instead of "he"). Law clerks should acquaint themselves with their judges' preference in regard to gender-specific language, and should keep in mind the federal judicial system's commitment to gender fairness.

D. Suggested Reference Material (Judges and Law Clerks)

Judicial Writing Manual (Federal Judicial Center 1991)

Ruggero J. Aldisert, Opinion Writing (West 1990)

Roy H. Copperud, American Usage and Style: The Consensus (Van Nostrand Reinhold 1980). This book presents the consensus of numerous usage authorities.

Webster's New World Dictionary (David B. Guralnik ed., 2d college ed. 1978) or The American Heritage Dictionary of the English Language (William Morris ed., 1978). As Copperud notes, these two dictionaries are "the most attentive to points of usage"; that is, they indicate levels of style or usage: nonstandard, informal, slang, vulgar, obsolete, and the like.

William Strunk, Jr. & E. B. White, The Elements of Style (E. B. White ed., 3d ed. 1979) (Macmillan). A classic. Particularly good for general advice on writing.

Richard C. Wydick, Plain English for Lawyers (2d ed. 1985) (Carolina Academic Press)

David Lambuth, The Golden Book of Writing (Penguin 1976). Similar to Strunk's book.

Henry W. Fowler, A Dictionary of Modern English Usage (E. Gowers ed., 2d ed. 1965) (Oxford University Press)

Wilson Follett, Modern American Usage: A Guide (J. Barzun ed., 1966) (Hill & Wang). More scholarly and detailed than Copperud (who, by the way, cites it frequently). Widely recognized as one of the premier usage authorities.

U.S. Government Printing Office Style Manual (rev. ed. 1973). A comprehensive guide to capitalization, spelling, compounding (e.g., "fact finder," "fact-finder," or "factfinder"), punctuation, abbreviations, numerals, and other matters of style.

Harbrace College Handbook (12th ed. 1993) (Harcourt Brace & Co.)

Webster's New Dictionary of Synonyms (G. & C. Merriam 1978). Splendid for distinguishing among synonyms (e.g., "language," "dialect," "tongue," "speech") and idiom (e.g., "let," "allow," "permit," "suffer," and "leave").

E. Supplemental Reference Material (Judges and Law Clerks)

Theodore M. Bernstein, The Careful Writer: A Modern Guide to English Usage (Atheneum 1977)

Morton S. Freeman, The Grammatical Lawyer (American Law Institute 1979)

John B. Bremner, Words on Words (Columbia University Press 1980).

Claire K. Cook, Line by Line: How to Improve Your Own Writing (Houghton Mifflin 1985)

Joseph M. Williams, Style: Toward Clarity & Grace (University of Chicago Press 1990)

Henry Weihofen, Legal Writing Style (West 1961)

Bryan A. Garner, A Dictionary of Modern Legal Usage (Oxford University Press 1987)

Bergen Evans & Cornelia Evans, A Dictionary of Contemporary American Usage (Random House 1957)

F. Specific Writing Assignments

1. Jury Instructions

Most district judges expect their law clerks to assume a major role in preparing proposed jury instructions. Some judges send a written copy of the instructions to the jury room with the jury, in which case instructions must be typed and ready before the end of the presentation of evidence. Judges who do not give the jury a written copy of the instructions may require a draft of them for a conference just before the parties rest. In all cases, the instructions must be prepared promptly.

The judge will indicate whether the case will be submitted to the jury for a general verdict or on special interrogatories. The use of special interrogatories may substantially affect the content of the charge. In addition, the judge will decide whether the trial of one or more issues is to be separated; for example, it is common in tort cases to try the liability issue separately and to ask the jury first to reach a verdict on this issue. If the jury decides for the defendant, it will be unnecessary for it to decide damages. If it decides for the plaintiff, the parties may reach a compromise without going to trial on damages.

The judge will have told trial counsel to submit requests for jury instructions. Most local court rules require that proposed instructions be submitted in duplicate at the beginning of the trial or at some earlier time. They may, of course, be supplemented if unforeseen matters arise during the course of the trial. Counsel are instructed that each paragraph of a requested instruction be typed on a separate piece of plain, white, letter-sized paper with the description at the top and numbered, for example, as Plaintiff's Requested Jury Instruction No. 1, with a citation of authority, such as a case or statute, at the end of the paragraph. (The citations are not read to the jury, but enable the judge or law clerk to determine quickly whether the requested instruction is correct.) Most likely, the judge will review counsel's requested instructions and will give the law clerk preliminary reactions. The judge may also instruct the law clerk to consult the judge's collection of standard or form instructions (often kept on the chambers computers). In addition, the law clerk should consult the record and the pretrial order, learn about the issues, and research relevant cases in order to prepare a draft. Substantive accuracy is of the utmost importance; erroneous jury instructions are a major cause of reversals or new trials.

Clear jury instructions require complete mastery of the subject and the use of plain language. Each instruction should be written in short, simple sentences, enumerating the elements of a violation, theory, or defense so that the jurors can approach a decision step-by-step. Names and facts should be inserted where appropriate, and the pertinent statute or legal rule should be quoted in part or paraphrased. The instruction should state the applicable rule in a way that makes sense and should be written in language that a high school student could understand.

Federal Rule of Civil Procedure 51 and Federal Rule of Criminal Procedure 30 require that, before closing arguments, the judge inform counsel which jury instructions will be given. Some judges hold a conference with counsel (usually in chambers, but on the record), discuss the proposed instructions, and permit counsel to argue for their requests. Other judges do not hold conferences, but deliver copies of their proposed instructions to all counsel and give counsel an opportunity to comment, object, or request additional instructions in writing.

In any event, before the jury is instructed, each counsel must be given an opportunity to make objections to the proposed instructions. This can be done in conference or in open court, but must be out of the presence of the jury. Some judges require counsel to write their objections directly on a copy of the proposed charge and then file this copy in the record for purposes of appellate review. If changes are made after a lawyer voices objections, the charge is re-typed and a copy of the charge as delivered is filed in the record. This procedure accurately records the instructions requested, any objections, and the charge delivered, in order to provide a complete and accurate record to the appellate court.

Once a final set of jury instructions has been prepared for a specific type of case, a copy should be retained in the judge's office file. Those instructions can be used as a starting point for the next case involving similar issues. Civil and criminal form jury instructions may be kept on computer diskettes or in separate loose-leaf binders. Form jury instructions for those issues that often arise may be photocopied for distribution to the attorneys before they prepare suggested charges. For example, in the Eastern District of Louisiana, the number of actions involving seamen, the Jones Act, and unseaworthiness is large enough to justify preparation of standard form instructions. Whatever the nature of the case, preserving a copy of the instructions can save future work.

The Federal Judicial Center published in 1987 the *Pattern Criminal Jury Instructions,* developed by the Subcommittee on Pattern Jury Instructions of the former Judicial Conference Committee on the Operation of the Jury System. In several circuits, committees of district judges have developed pattern or model jury charges that serve as a helpful guide. Each judge in those circuits has a copy of the pattern charges; most judges use them as a starting point.

For forms previously used by other district judges, many judges consult Devitt and Blackmar, *Federal Jury Practice and Instructions* (West Publishing Co. 4th ed. 1987). Another comprehensive work is *Modern Federal Jury Instructions* (Bender 1984), edited by, among others, Judge Leonard B. Sand of the Southern District of New York, and updated frequently. In antitrust cases, it may be useful to consult the American Bar Association's *Sample Jury Instructions in Civil Antitrust Cases* (1987). The ABA Litigation Section has prepared *Model Jury Instructions for Business Tort Litigation* (1980). In addition, many specialized texts include forms for jury charges in those legal fields.

2. Memoranda of Law or Fact

A memorandum is an informal document intended to communicate the results of a research assignment or a summary of a case. All memoranda should indicate the following:

- The person by whom the memo was prepared (some judges want the law clerk to use initials only);

- The date it was prepared; and

- The type of memo, or a short summary of the subject discussed.

Some of the most common memoranda are

a) The bench memorandum

This is a document prepared by an appellate law clerk for the judge to use during oral argument. Most judges want bench memos to be brief, often only a page or two, and do not expect a significant amount of independent research by the law clerk. The bench memo is most often a summary of the briefs of the parties, together with (when requested) analysis of the validity of the respective positions of the parties and identification of issues that require further inquiry.

One commonly used organizational format for a bench memo contains the following:

- the docket number, a short caption of the case, and names of members of the panel;

- the district court and the name of the judge from whom the appeal is taken;

- a statement of the case, reflecting how the case arose, the procedural history and status, the trial court's ruling, and which party appealed;

- a brief statement of the facts of the case;

- a statement of the issues raised by the parties;

- a summary of the arguments raised by the parties;

- matters that should be clarified, expanded, or explained during oral argument; and

- if requested by the judge, the law clerk's views on the merits of the case, supported by analysis and explanation, and recommendations on disposition of the case. (Some judges do not wish their law clerks to express any views; others discourage any conclusory language until after the case has been argued and thoroughly researched.)

b) The statement of facts

Frequently, a judge wants the facts in a particular case, or the facts relating to a specific issue, summarized in writing. In an appellate court, the sources for this kind of memo are the briefs and appendix or record excerpts. In a trial court, the sources are the case file, trial exhibits, the law clerk's notes taken during hearings, and, when necessary, the court reporter's notes or transcripts.

In preparing a statement of facts, the law clerk should strive for accuracy and objectivity, and, if there are disputed factual issues, should present the evidence supporting each position. The law clerk should neither allow a personal opinion to shade the statement of facts nor present a partisan view of the evidence. A narrative statement of the facts, arranged chronologically, is usually the easiest to understand. Depending on the status of the case, the judge may wish the law clerk to express a view about how any conflicts in the evidence should be resolved.

c) The single-issue memorandum

The need for a memo dealing with a single issue may arise from inadequate preparation by counsel, an unexpected development during trial, or the judge's wish to pursue an aspect of the case not fully developed by the attorneys. This memo may have to be prepared under extreme time pressure during trial, but nevertheless must be completed with accuracy and care.

d) The full-case memorandum

This type of memo is usually preliminary to an opinion, and, unless otherwise instructed, the law clerk should approach it in that manner. It is usually better to overwrite this kind of memo, including facts of borderline relevancy and legal research that, although not directly on point, may have some bearing on the outcome of the case—it is easier to delete unnecessary material than to insert material omitted from an earlier draft. Some judges like this memo in the form of an opinion.

Legal problems often repeat themselves. After completing a research memorandum, or upon reading a brief submitted to the court that is unusually thorough, the law clerk should file a copy in the judge's legal memoranda files for future use. Such files can be an invaluable resource and prevent needless duplication of effort. Some judges maintain these files on computer disk, in expandable folders, or in manila folders filed in alphabetical order in a file drawer (labeled by subject).

3. Resolution of Motions in Trial Courts

The resolution of motions often constitutes a substantial part of the trial court's work on a case. Some motions may require an opinion equivalent in substance and length to a final opinion after trial. In most, the judge may write only a short opinion or order, dictate reasons into the record, or simply indicate disposition with a single word: "Granted" or "Denied." The law clerk is usually the member of the judge's staff charged with responsibility for knowing which motions are pending, what memoranda or other pleadings have been filed with respect to each motion, and the status of each motion. The judge will instruct the law clerk as to the type of memorandum or order indicated. Motion management is discussed in more detail in Chapter 3 *supra*.

Some judges want their law clerks to prepare a memorandum on every motion. Others require memoranda only on certain matters or for certain types of cases.

If required to prepare a memorandum, the law clerk should first examine the briefs or memoranda from both the moving party and the opposition. The legal standard or rule that applies is often fairly clear; the difficulty is in applying the rule to the facts. The facts are almost always incompletely—sometimes even deceptively—presented. Each party's version must be examined and compared, and then checked against the exhibits, declarations, or other materials in the record.

The law clerk should find samples of predecessors' memos and use them as guides. There is no one style or format for memos on motions, but certain features are common:

- Name and number of the case, perhaps the category of case (e.g., antitrust, diversity tort case), the date of the memo, and the writer's initials.

- Statement of the nature of the motion or motions now under consideration, identifying the moving party.

- Recommended disposition, summarized.

- Statement of facts and procedural posture. This should include a description of the parties and their relationships to one another, key events, and a notation of facts in dispute. The memo should indicate the source of the facts stated, particularly when they are controverted or perhaps intentionally vague, such as the paragraph of the complaint, the identification of the relevant affidavit and paragraph number, or the number of the exhibit from which the fact stated is derived.

- Discussion of the parties' chief arguments, the legal standard set by controlling statutes, rules, or precedent, and a succinct explanation of the law clerk's reasons for recommending a particular result on each point.

- Some judges may wish to have a draft of a proposed order or judgment disposing of the matter along the lines recommended by the law clerk.

When the memo is completed, the law clerk should keep one copy and give another to the judge with the case work file.

Law clerks should avoid two common errors: (1) failing to pay attention to the procedural status of the case, and (2) writing a law review style piece rather than a memorandum that meets the judge's needs.

4. Memos for Criminal Motions

The law clerk is not usually required to prepare a memo for each motion in a criminal case. In some districts, motions are made in an omnibus pleading. In others, they may be made separately, but without a predetermined schedule because the Speedy Trial Act requires that a criminal defendant be brought to trial within seventy days of the initiation of proceedings, and there is little time for briefing schedules.

Before writing a memorandum, the law clerk should check with the courtroom deputy (or, if the judge's policy permits, with opposing counsel) to determine whether opposing counsel will oppose the motion. Many suppression motions, for example, are not contested. The judge may handle last-minute evidentiary or procedural motions personally, as they often surface first during the pretrial conference. When a memo must be written, the process is essentially the same as that used in preparing memos in civil cases.

5. Findings of Fact and Conclusions of Law

A district judge who sits as the trier of fact in an evidentiary hearing or trial may prepare either a conventional opinion or findings of fact (a statement in separately numbered paragraphs of each material fact that the judge concludes was proved) and conclusions of law (these follow the findings of fact, and state in separate paragraphs the principles of law the judge finds applicable to the facts).

Arranging findings of fact and conclusions of law in separately numbered paragraphs (each consisting of one or two relatively brief declarative statements) helps the parties understand the opinion and makes appellate review easier. The judge may direct the law clerk to prepare a draft of either the opinion or the findings of fact and conclusions of law.

In some cases, the court requires plaintiff's counsel to prepare proposed findings of fact and conclusions of law and requires defense counsel to respond. Other judges may require each counsel to prepare a separate proposal. The court reviews the proposals and makes necessary revisions or additions before adopting any of them.

If proposed findings of fact are based on transcribed testimony (either by deposition or of the trial), the court may insert citations to page numbers of the various transcripts at the end of each paragraph of conclusions of fact, and the law clerk may be asked to review those citations. The law clerk may also be given the task of reviewing legal authorities cited by the parties in their trial briefs to determine whether the proposed conclusions of law are correct.

6. District Court Orders

Federal Rule of Civil Procedure 58 provides that "upon a general verdict of a jury, or upon a decision by the court that a party shall receive only a sum certain or costs or that all relief shall be denied, the clerk [of court], unless the court otherwise orders, shall forthwith prepare, sign, and enter the judgment without awaiting any direction by the court." If, however, the court grants other relief, or the jury returns a special verdict or a general verdict accompanied by answers to interrogatories, the clerk of court prepares a form of judgment and "the court shall promptly approve the form of the judgment, and the clerk [of court] shall thereupon enter it." The rule also provides that "[a]ttorneys shall not submit forms of judgment except upon direction of the court, and these directions shall not be given as a matter of course."

Routine orders are usually prepared in the office of the clerk of court. In some cases, however, it may be necessary for the court to prepare an order that states the relief to be granted. These orders are prepared in the judge's chambers and are sometimes drafted by the law clerk. In some courts, judges direct the prevailing party to prepare an order and submit it to opposing counsel for approval.

Most courts have a standardized format for orders, and the judge's secretary will be familiar with that format. This usually includes the name of the court, the docket number of the case, the caption of the case with the names of the parties, and a descriptive title indicating the nature of the order. A paragraph should be included stating the date of the hearing (if any), appearances of counsel, and the nature of the matter decided by the order.

An order has two functional parts: (1) the factual or legal basis for the determination; and (2) a statement that tells the parties what action the court is taking and what they must do as a result of that action.

No specific language is required to make an order effective. Use simple and unambiguous language. The purpose of the order is to tell the person to whom the order is directed precisely what to do and to allow others to determine whether that person has done it correctly and completely.

a) Reviewing orders and judgments submitted by the parties
The parties may submit a proposed order or judgment for the district judge's signature in the following circumstances: The judge ruled from the bench on a legal matter and asked the prevailing party to submit an appropriate order for the judge's signature; the judge de-

cided a nonjury case, announced from the bench his or her findings or reasons and grounds, and asked the prevailing party to submit an appropriate judgment; or the parties stipulated to a result in a particular case, with or without the judge's prior involvement, and submitted a proposed order, accompanied by their stipulation, for the judge's approval and signature. In other cases, pursuant to Federal Rule of Civil Procedure 58, the clerk of court may submit a prepared form of judgment for court approval.

When these documents arrive at chambers, a law clerk is usually responsible for their detailed review and should take the following steps:

- If the order or judgment is submitted after the judge has made a determination in court with all parties present, the law clerk should check to be certain that the losing party agrees that the order or judgment conforms to the judge's decision. Such approval is usually indicated by the signatures of counsel for the losing party (e.g., "Approved as to form. Signed J. Attorney, Counsel for Defendant").

- If the parties agreed or stipulated to the decision, with or without the judge's prior involvement, the law clerk should confirm that the submitted order or judgment is accompanied by the stipulation, signed by the parties, and the order or judgment itself has been approved as to *form* and *substance* by all parties.

- The law clerk should check the substance of the order or judgment to be certain that it complies with the judge's directions on the stipulation or agreement.

7. Opinions

Opinion writing involves four basic steps:

- *Researching.* To write a draft of an opinion, a law clerk must first become thoroughly familiar with the case. Read the briefs and the record or case file, complete all necessary legal research, and discuss the proposed opinion with the judge, examining the structure, the rationale, and the result to be reached. Frequently, additional research is necessary as the opinion is drafted.

- *Listening to tape recordings of oral arguments.* Many courts of appeals record appellate oral arguments. The clerk of court makes a tape recording of all arguments, and the relevant tape is provided to the judge assigned to write the opinion. Even a law clerk who attended oral argument may want to listen to the tape before beginning to draft an opinion in order to refresh his or her memory concerning the issues, the judge's questions to counsel, and counsel's responses. Moreover, a law clerk may be assigned the task of drafting an opinion in a case in which oral argument was heard before the beginning of the law clerk's tenure. In such circumstances, listening to the tape is essential. In the district court, an audio recording of the trial may assist in reviewing the issues or preparing a draft opinion.

  Many court reporters tape-record the trial as an aid in preparing the transcript and may be willing to release this audio record to the law clerk. For those courtrooms in which audio recording is the official court reporting method, the clerk of court can provide the tape recording. Oral arguments on motions or legal questions in district court are usually not transcribed and do not ordinarily form part of the record. Unless the attorneys or the judge asks the court reporter to take down such oral arguments, no record will be available.

- *Planning the opinion.*

  - Write a clear statement of the facts and legal issues presented in the case.

  - Determine which issues must be decided. If the case turns on a procedural issue, any discussion of substantive issues raised by the parties may be gratuitous. Occasionally, if the same result would have been reached after considering the substantive issues, so stating may strengthen the opinion.

  - Determine which parts of the opinion raise issues to be treated in detail. If there is a circuit decision directly on point, a lengthy analysis of the precedents and principles related to that particular issue has little value.

- Outline the opinion. In opinions, as in any other kind of writing, a good outline will help the writer produce a clear, complete, and well-organized product.

- *Writing the opinion.*

  - *The introduction (opening paragraph).* The introduction should establish clearly who the parties are and, if the case is on appeal, what agency or court decisions are being reviewed. In addition, many judges like to state at the outset the principal issues and the decision made by the writing court. This practice has the advantage of immediately informing the reader of the result in the case. Illustrative is the opinion of the Supreme Court in *First English Evangelical Lutheran Church v. County of Los Angeles*, 482 U.S. 304 (1987), written by Chief Justice William Rehnquist, which begins:

    > In this case the California Court of Appeals held that a landowner who claims that his property has been "taken" by a land-use regulation may not recover damages for the time before it is finally determined that the regulation constitutes a "taking" of his property. We disagree, and conclude that in these circumstances the Fifth and Fourteenth Amendments to the United States Constitution would require compensation for that period.

  - *The facts.* State the facts developed at the trial or in the record in chronological order. Do this in a narrative style, using short sentences. Recite all of the relevant facts but omit everything else. Avoid verbatim quotations of excerpts from the pleadings or the transcript. In an appellate opinion, this part of the opinion may conclude with a résumé of the trial court's or agency's reasons for its decision and a statement of the issues on appeal.

  - *Applicable law.* Discuss the legal principles applicable to the case. (In appellate opinions, the applicable law usually includes the standard of review.) Avoid lengthy quotations from cases or treatises. Cite the authorities for these principles, but avoid string citations.

    Meritless points do not require detailed discussion. Many lawyers will present a smorgasbord of issues in a brief, hoping that the judge may find some tempting morsel among the offerings. In such cases, mention these issues so the lawyers will know they were noticed and simply say they are without merit (e.g., "considering the testimony of the informant, the argument that the evidence was insufficient to warrant conviction merits no discussion").

- *Disposition.* Apply the legal principles to the facts.

- *Closing.* Close with a specific statement of the disposition: judgment is rendered for the plaintiff in the amount of $X; the judgment appealed is affirmed, revised and rendered, or reversed and the case is remanded, with appropriate instructions to the lower court. These instructions should not leave the lower court any doubt as to what is required on remand.

- *Footnotes.* When reviewing a heavily footnoted opinion, the reader's eyes must constantly move from text to footnotes and back again. This is distracting and wastes time. For this reason, some judges object to any footnotes. Others use footnotes only for citations. Most judges use them to expand on the text of an opinion, to explain an inference in the opinion, or to discuss authorities. The law clerk should follow the judge's practice.

- *General suggestions.* Remember that this is a judicial opinion, not an essay or a law review article. Avoid personalized argument (and abuse of other judges). Write simply. Stick to the active voice where possible. Avoid excessive use of adjectives and adverbs. Make the meaning clear by using verbs and nouns. Do not clutter the opinion by citing every case you have read. Pare the message to its essentials. The opinion should cogently state the court's decision and the basis for it.

G. Correspondence

Some district judges prohibit law clerks from corresponding with lawyers; the judges either draft their own correspondence, direct their law clerks or secretaries to prepare drafts of correspondence for their signature, or delegate correspondence entirely to their secretaries. Other judges, however, direct their law clerks to correspond with lawyers from time to time on a variety of matters, such as inquiring about the progress of a case, scheduling a trial or hearing date, or requesting compliance with the court's procedural requirements. The judge's secretary can provide a sample of letters written or approved by the judge. The law clerk should refer to these samples, or consult the secretary, regarding technical matters such as the form of the letter heading and opening address.

The law clerk and secretary may find the following suggestions relating to court correspondence helpful:

- Let the reader know immediately what the letter refers to. In a large law firm, someone must sort the mail to see that it is delivered to the proper lawyer, and once that lawyer receives it someone must determine to which case the letter relates. You can simplify these tasks by addressing your letter to a specific lawyer rather than to a firm and by placing the case title and docket number near the top of the page.

- Let the reader know why the law clerk or secretary, rather than the judge, is writing. A lawyer may wonder why a staff member is giving him or her instructions or requesting information. Therefore, use a simple introductory phrase such as "Judge Smith has asked me to advise you . . ." or "Judge Smith has ordered . . . ."

- Remember that, although the letter may bear the law clerk's or secretary's signature, it is written on behalf of the judge. Excessive formality is not required, but undue familiarity is inappropriate.

- Get to the point. For example, it may be helpful to the reader to know that this is in response to a letter that the addressee wrote earlier. This can be handled simply by starting your letter, "In response to your letter of May 1, Judge Smith has asked me to advise you that matters of this kind must be raised by written motion served upon opposing counsel."

- Remember that the law clerk, like the judge, is a neutral party dealing with advocates. Unless the judge specifically directs otherwise, the law clerk should send copies of case-related correspondence to all counsel in the case. Even though the law clerk may believe that a letter is of significance only to the addressee, the court has an obligation to avoid ex parte communications.

1. Official Business Envelopes

Court envelopes and postage meters should be used only for court business—they should not be used to mail personal items.

The U.S. Postal Service now requires all federal agencies to use postage meters and is committed to a successful conversion from indicia envelopes to metered postage by September 30, 1994. All outgoing mail from courts (including units and offices) must bear a postage meter imprint or other prepaid postage by this date.

2. Juror Letters

Some district judges send a letter to each of the jurors after service on a given case, expressing the court's appreciation. If the judge follows this practice, the office files will contain sample letters. The jury clerk can furnish a list of the jurors and their addresses. If the judge directs the law clerk to prepare such a letter, the law clerk should select a form for the letter, or compose a new one, and send a letter to each member of the jury, including alternates. If a particular juror serves a second or third time, the law clerk should make sure that the letter is different each time.

3. Prisoner Correspondence

Prisoners and persons who have been convicted and are awaiting sentence frequently write district and appellate judges. The problems of a prisoner represented by counsel are handled the same way as those of any other litigant. If the prisoner is proceeding pro se, however, the correspondence may require special attention.

a) Prisoner mail in general

Prisoners write judges for a variety of reasons. Because the prisoners frequently have little formal education, the law clerk must read letters carefully to determine whether, in fact, the prisoner is requesting legal relief. For example, a letter may, in substance, request a reduction of sentence without clearly articulating that request. A good rule is to give the writer the benefit of the doubt and to assume that the letter requests judicial relief. If, after careful reading, the letter is still unclear, the law clerk should take the matter up with the judge.

Some letters ask the judge for a transfer to another penal institution. Only the Bureau of Prisons has authority to grant this type of request. The judge may have a form letter to use in responding to such requests. If not, the law clerk should prepare a letter instructing the prisoner about the procedure that must be followed, and keep an extra copy to use as a future form.

Other letters may ask the judge for a variety of things. If it is not possible to take action on the request at once, the law clerk should prepare for the judge's signature a short response acknowledging receipt of the letter.

If the letter does not request relief that the court has the power to grant, then the judge may wish to follow this course:

- If the letter is from a prisoner, the reply letter should state that federal law prohibits judges from giving legal advice and should suggest that the prisoner communicate with a lawyer. If the prisoner persists in writing the judge, or indicates financial inability to retain counsel, the judge may refer the writer to an agency that regularly handles prisoner complaints or may forward the letter itself to such an agency (e.g., the Staff Counsel for Inmates, Texas Department of Corrections).

- If the letter comes from a local jail where the person is being held on a pending federal charge, and the request appears to be reasonable (e.g., "I need to get out for a few hours to make financial arrangements to keep from losing my home while I am in jail"), the judge may ask the marshal to help the person.

  The law clerk should *never* write anything in a letter that would give a prisoner false hope or compromise the position of the court.

b) Other prisoner correspondence

Other prisoner correspondence will generally fall into one of four categories: pleas for a reduction of sentence, requests for habeas corpus, complaints about violation of civil rights, and pleas for intercession with the Parole Commission or the Sentencing Commission.

Most prisoner petitions are filed in forma pauperis. A petitioner who seeks to proceed in this fashion must obtain leave of court after filing an affidavit showing inability to pay costs. The office of the clerk of court will supply forms for this purpose. If the prisoner has some money, the court may require a modest payment, less than the usual amount of fees, to assure the petitioner's good faith.

Some pro se petitions are prepared with the assistance of law schools or legal organizations, but even when such assistance has been provided, the organization will usually not provide counsel to try the case. The Criminal Justice Act (18 U.S.C. § 3006A) permits a court to appoint compensated counsel to represent an indigent petitioner in section 2254 and section 2255 cases, though counsel may receive substantially less than the usual fees for similar services. The pro se petitioner may file a motion for the appointment of counsel. If so, the court must decide whether the case is likely to be of sufficient merit and complexity to warrant appointment of counsel. The court may also appoint counsel sua sponte if it concludes that the interests of justice so require.

There is no provision for the payment of counsel in section 1983 (state action) cases or in *Bivens*-type (federal action) cases.

c) Pleas for reduction of sentence

(1) *Guideline-sentenced offenders.* Federal Rule of Criminal Procedure 35(a) directs the district court to correct a sentence, on remand, imposed under the Sentencing Guidelines (see *supra* section 3-2.H) if, on appeal, the appellate court determines that the sentence was illegal, the result of an incorrect guideline application, or an unreasonable departure from the guidelines. Federal Rule of Criminal Procedure 35(b) authorizes the district court, on motion of the government, to lower a sentence to reflect the offender's "subsequent, substantial assistance in the investigation or prosecution of another" offender.

Except as noted below, the Rules of Criminal Procedure provide the district court with no other authority to correct improper sentences or sentences imposed in an illegal manner. However, offenders may seek the same relief by filing a habeas corpus-type motion under 28 U.S.C. § 2255.

(2) *Pre-guideline sentenced offenders.* Federal Rule of Criminal Procedure 35 took effect on November 1, 1987, at the same time as the Sentencing Guidelines. The former Rule 35 provided the court substantially greater authority to correct or reduce sentences. A statute enacted in 1987 made it clear that the old rule applies to offenders sentenced under the pre-guideline system. Because several years may elapse until the final appellate disposition of cases involving pre-guideline sentences, courts may be receiving old Rule 35(b) motions for some time. Additionally, prisoners sentenced under the guidelines may nevertheless be unaware of the rule change and incorrectly seek reductions under the old rule.

Former Federal Rule of Criminal Procedure 35 provided:

- Correction of Sentence. The court may correct an illegal sentence at any time and may correct a sentence imposed in an illegal manner within the time provided herein for the reduction of sentence.

- Reduction of Sentence. A motion to reduce a sentence may be made, or the court may reduce a sentence without motion within 120 days after the sentence is imposed or probation is revoked, or within 120 days after receipt by the court of a mandate issued upon affirmance of the judgment or dismissal of the appeal, or within 120 days after entry of any order or judgment of the Supreme Court denying review of, or having the effect of upholding, a judgment of conviction or probation revocation.

If this rule were read literally, it would require the judge to make the reduction within 120 days and it would not suffice that the motion itself had been filed by then. Every circuit confronted with this issue, however, has held that it is sufficient if the motion is filed within 120 days, provided the judge acts with reasonable promptness thereafter.

If the request is in the form of a letter written by the prisoner, the law clerk should carry out the following steps:

- Determine whether the writer seeks a reduction of sentence, and, if so, whether old Rule 35 applies and whether the request has been made in timely fashion;

- Type "MOTION FOR REDUCTION OF SENTENCE" at the top of the letter (if the letter does not already contain a similar caption); and

- Staple the letter and envelope together, and file it with the office of the clerk of court as soon as possible, taking steps to see that the letter–motion has the court file number on the face of the letter.

After the letter–motion has been docketed and filed by the clerk's office, it will be returned to the judge's chambers via the courtroom deputy clerk. If old Rule 35(b) does not apply to the prisoner, or if the motion has not been timely filed, the judge has no authority to grant relief. If this is the case, the judge may instruct the law clerk to prepare an order denying any relief and stating the reason. The law clerk should find a form in the office files or prepare one to be used in the future. If a motion for reduction of sentence is filed by the defendant's lawyer, it is treated like any other motion.

If the motion was timely filed, the law clerk should write a brief memorandum stating the basis for the request and the relief sought. The law clerk should attach the memorandum to the prisoner's sentencing file and give it to the judge for consideration. The judge may decide to deny relief under the discretionary authority granted by old Federal Rule of Criminal Procedure 35(b) or to grant some form of relief. In either case, the judge may direct the law clerk to prepare an appropriate order. If the law clerk does not find a form in the office files, it may be helpful to prepare one for future use.

d) Habeas corpus-like complaints

These should be handled like a formal habeas corpus proceeding. Most district courts require the prisoner who files such a complaint to complete a special form that makes clear the complaint and the relief sought. If the prisoner–petitioner has not done so, the clerk of court should be asked to send this form to the prisoner–petitioner.

After receiving the form, the clerk of court opens a record, as the form constitutes a petition and formally initiates a case.

e) Civil rights complaints

Requests for civil rights relief made by prisoners (and others—for example, persons seeking relief from discrimination under Title VII), though not formal complaints, should be filed and processed. The letter should be sent to the clerk of court to open a file. In some courts, the complaint may be referred to a magistrate judge for initial examination so that, if it is found frivolous, it may be dismissed summarily without requiring an answer. The law clerk must ascertain the procedure the judge wishes to have followed.

f) Pleas for intercession with the Parole Commission, the Sentencing Commission, or the Department of Justice's pardon attorney

The release dates for prisoners who were not sentenced under the Sentencing Guidelines are determined by the U.S. Parole Commission. Prisoners sentenced under the guidelines may petition the Sentencing Commission to modify the guidelines used in determining their sentence on the basis of changed circumstances unrelated to the defendant (28 U.S.C. § 994(s)). Judges may receive letters from defendants asking the judge to intercede with either commission. Similarly, judges may receive correspondence from defendants seeking intercession with the Office of the Pardon Attorney of the Department of Justice. The judge probably has a form letter that refers the complainant to the appropriate commission. If it appears that the letter is in effect a habeas corpus petition or civil rights complaint (e.g., if the prisoner asserts that the commission has denied him due process), it should be handled as stated above.

§ 7-3. Proofreading and Checking of Citations

The need for accuracy in every document issued by the court cannot be overemphasized. A document that contains misspelled words or inaccurate citations indicates a lack of care in its final preparation. Every document must be proofread meticulously both for substantive correctness and to eliminate typographical and grammatical errors.

Proofreading demands painstaking care. In checking citations, the law clerk must be certain of the following:

- The cases cited in the opinion stand for the proposition of law for which they are cited;

- The parties' names are spelled correctly and the volume, court, page number, and year of the decision are correctly given; and

- The style of the citation is consistent with the style usually followed by the court. (Most judges use *The Blue Book: A Uniform System of Citation* as a guide. Others may use *The Chicago Manual of Legal Citation.*)

It is a good idea for a law clerk other than the one responsible for an opinion to check the citations in the last draft of the opinion. A fresh pair of eyes is more likely to catch errors—occasional errors occur no matter how carefully the judge and the law clerk try to avoid them.

A. Checking an Opinion

A law clerk may be asked to review an opinion drafted by the judge. As a preliminary matter, the law clerk should verify the following:

- The court has jurisdiction;

- The procedural status of the case is correctly stated;

- The court's ruling—the "holding" of the opinion—is stated clearly and succinctly;

- The facts supporting the losing party have been stated;

- The arguments of the losing party have been stated and adequately addressed;

- The cases cited stand for the propositions for which they are asserted; and

- The conclusions are supported by clear reasoning and authorities.

The law clerk should also seek to eliminate any errors that may have occurred in preparation. An opinion may be checked by following these steps:

- Check the formal elements

  - Compare the case title to the docket sheet in the clerk's office;

  - Compare the listing of counsel who appeared in the case to the briefs and minute order or submission order in the file (in appellate courts, this is usually done in the office of the clerk of court); and

  - If the hearing was before a multiple-judge panel, compare the judges' names and the order in which they are listed to the records of the clerk of court or the judges' notes.

- Check all factual statements

  - Check all factual statements against the original transcripts, if any, and documents. Do not rely on factual representations in the briefs or appendix. Factual statements may be supported by citations to the original depositions, transcripts, or exhibits in the following manner: "(Smith dep., p. 10)";

  - Proofread, word for word, each direct quotation from an exhibit or a witness's testimony;

  - Be certain all omissions from quotations have been indicated by ellipses or asterisks; and

  - Verify all dates and numbers.

- Check the accuracy of citations and quotations.

- Review the briefs to be certain all issues have been covered.

B. Final Proofreading

After an opinion has been checked and edited, the working draft will have interlineations, marginal inserts, and strikeouts, and may well have been cut into pieces that have been stapled or pasted together or assembled by a word processor. Proofread the final draft to be certain that it is identical to the working draft. When a word processor is used, it is particularly easy to overlook an inadvertent omission or unintended inclusion.

1. Galleys

The slip opinions of many courts are printed by commercial contract printers. Before formal publication, such printers provide the court with galley proofs that must be proofread. In those circuits for which it is the official printer, West Publishing Company sends the slip opinions without providing galley proofs in advance. *See supra* section 7-1A. Proofreading the slip opinion is usually the law clerk's responsibility.

Proofreading is dull work, but it is important and must be done with care and accuracy. It is most accurate when one law clerk reads aloud from the copy being verified to another law clerk who follows on the correct, master copy.

The reader should read all punctuation, spell out all proper nouns and foreign or technical words and phrases, and indicate whether numbers are spelled out or in figures. This technique minimizes the risk that typographical errors will be missed. Standardized proofreader's symbols can be found in most dictionaries. The use of these symbols indicates to the printer the changes to be made.

Appendix

Code of Conduct for Law Clerks

Canon 1

A Law Clerk Should Uphold the Integrity and Independence of the Judiciary and the Office

An independent and honorable judiciary is indispensable to justice in our society. A law clerk should observe high standards of conduct so that the integrity and independence of the judiciary may be preserved. The provisions of this Code should be construed and applied to further that objective. The standards of this Code shall not affect or preclude other more stringent standards required by law, by court order, or by direction of the appointing judge.

Canon 2

A Law Clerk Should Avoid Impropriety and the Appearance of Impropriety in All Activities

A law clerk should not engage in any activities that would put into question the propriety of the law clerk's conduct in carrying out the duties of the office. A law clerk should not allow family, social, or other relationships to influence official conduct or judgment. A law clerk should not lend the prestige of the office to advance the private interests of others; nor should the law clerk convey or permit others to convey the impression that they are in a special position to influence the law clerk.

Canon 3

A Law Clerk Should Perform the Duties of the Office Impartially and Diligently

The official duties of a law clerk take precedence over all other activities. Official duties include all the duties of the office prescribed by law, resolution of the Judicial Conference of the United States, the court in which the law clerk serves, and the appointing judge. In the performance of these duties, the following standards apply:

171

A. A law clerk should respect and comply with the law and should conduct himself or herself at all times in a manner that promotes public confidence in the integrity and impartiality of the judiciary and of the office.

B. A law clerk should maintain professional competence in the profession. A law clerk should be dignified, courteous, and fair to all persons with whom the law clerk deals in the law clerk's official capacity. A law clerk should diligently discharge the responsibilities of the office. A law clerk should bear in mind the obligation to treat fairly and courteously the general public as well as the legal profession.

C. The relationship between judge and law clerk is essentially a confidential one. A law clerk should abstain from public comment about a pending or impending proceeding in the court in which the law clerk serves. A law clerk should never disclose to any person any confidential information received in the course of the law clerk's duties, nor should the law clerk employ such information for personal gain. This subsection does not prohibit a law clerk from making public statements in the course of official duties to the extent authorized by the appointing judge.

D. A law clerk should inform the appointing judge of any circumstance or activity of the law clerk that might serve as a basis for disqualification of the judge, e.g., a prospective employment relation with a law firm, association of the law clerk's spouse with a law firm or litigant, etc.

Canon 4

A Law Clerk May Engage in Activities to Improve the Law, the Legal System, and the Administration of Justice

A law clerk, subject to the proper performance of official duties, may engage in the following law-related activities:

A. A law clerk may speak, write, lecture, teach, and participate in other activities concerning the law, the legal system, and the administration of justice.

B. A law clerk may serve as a member, officer, or director of an organization or governmental agency devoted to the improvement of the law, the legal system, or the administration of justice. A law clerk may assist such an organization in raising funds and may participate in their management and investment but should not personally participate in public fund-raising activities. A law clerk may make recommendations to public and private fund-granting agencies on projects and programs concerning the law, the legal profession, and the administration of justice.

C. A law clerk may promote the development of professional organizations and foster the interchange of technical information and experience with others in the profession. A law clerk may make himself or herself available to the public at large for speaking engagements and public appearances designed to enhance the public's knowledge of the operation of the court system.

Canon 5

A Law Clerk Should Regulate Extra-Official Activities to Minimize the Risk of Conflict with Official Duties

A. *Avocational Activities*. A law clerk may write, lecture, teach, and speak on nonlegal subjects and engage in the arts, sports, and other social and recreational activities, if such avocational activities do not detract from the dignity of the office or interfere with the performance of official duties.

B. *Civic and Charitable Activities*. A law clerk may participate in civic and charitable activities that do not detract from the dignity of the office or interfere with the performance of official duties. A law clerk may serve as an officer, director, trustee, or nonlegal advisor of an educational, religious, charitable, fraternal, or civic organization and solicit funds for any such organization subject to the following limitations:

(1) A law clerk should not use or permit the use of the prestige of the office in the solicitation of funds.

(2) A law clerk should not solicit court personnel to contribute to or participate in any civic or charitable activity, but may call their attention to a general fund-raising campaign such as the Combined Federal Campaign and the United Way.

(3) A law clerk should not solicit funds from lawyers or persons likely to come before the court in which the law clerk serves.

C. *Financial Activities.*

(1) A law clerk should refrain from financial and business dealings that tend to detract from the dignity of the office, interfere with the proper performance of official duties, exploit the law clerk's position, or involve the law clerk in frequent transactions with individuals likely to come in contact with the law clerk or the court in which the law clerk serves. During the law clerkship, a law clerk may seek and obtain employment to commence after the completion of the law clerkship; if any law firm, lawyer, or entity with whom a law clerk has been employed or is seeking or has obtained future employment appears in any matter pending before the appointing judge, the law clerk should promptly bring this fact to the attention of the appointing judge, and the extent of the law clerk's performance of duties in connection with such matter should be determined by the appointing judge.

(2) Neither a law clerk nor a member of the law clerk's household should solicit or accept a gift, bequest, favor, or loan from anyone except for—

(a) a gift incident to a public testimonial, books, tapes, and other resource materials supplied by publishers on a complimentary basis for official use, or an invitation to the law clerk and a family member to attend a bar-related function or an activity devoted to the improvement of the law, the legal system, or the administration of justice;

(b)   a gift, award, or benefit incident to the business, profession, or other separate activity of a spouse or family member of a law clerk residing in the law clerk's household, including gifts, awards, and benefits for the use of both the spouse or other family member and the law clerk (as spouse or family member), provided the gift, award, or benefit could not reasonably be perceived as intended to influence the law clerk in the performance of official duties;

(c)   ordinary social hospitality;

(d)   a gift from a relative or friend for a special occasion, such as a wedding, anniversary, or birthday, if the gift is fairly commensurate with the occasion and the relationship;

(e)   a gift, bequest, favor, or loan from a relative or close personal friend whose appearance or interest in a case would in any event require that the law clerk take no official action with respect to the case;

(f)   a loan from a lending institution in its regular course of business on the same terms generally available to persons who are not law clerks;

(g)   a scholarship or fellowship awarded on the same terms and based on the same criteria applied to other applicants; or

(h)   any other gift, bequest, favor, or loan, only if:

(i)   the donor has not sought and is not seeking to do business with the court or other entity served by the law clerk; or

(ii)   the donor is not a party or other person who has had or is likely to have any interest in the performance of the law clerk's official duties.

(3)   A law clerk should report the value of any gift, bequest, favor, or loan as required by statute or by the Judicial Conference of the United States.

D. *Practice of Law.* A law clerk shall not practice law in any federal, state, or local court, or undertake to perform legal services for any private client in return for remuneration. This prohibition, however, shall not be construed to preclude the performance of routine legal work necessary to the management of the personal affairs of the law clerk or a member of the law clerk's family, so long as:

   (1) Such work is done without compensation or for nominal compensation;

   (2) It does not require any act, including the entry of an appearance in a court of the United States, that would suggest that the position of law clerk is being misused, that preferential treatment is being sought by virtue of the holding of the position, or that would otherwise be inconsistent with the law clerk's primary responsibility to the court; and

   (3) So long as such activity does not have actual conflict or appear in conflict with court duties or will not reflect adversely on the court or create the appearance of impropriety.

A law clerk should ascertain and observe any limitations imposed by the appointing judge or the court on which the appointing judge serves concerning the practice of law by a former law clerk before the judge or the court.

Canon 6

A Law Clerk Should Regularly File Any Required Reports of Compensation Received for All Extra-Official Activities

A law clerk may receive compensation and reimbursement of expenses for all extra-official activities permitted by this Code, if the source of such payments does not influence or give the appearance of influencing the law clerk in the performance of official duties or otherwise give the appearance of impropriety, subject to the following restrictions:

A. *Compensation.* Compensation should not exceed a reasonable amount nor should it exceed that normally received by others for the same activity.

B. *Expense Reimbursement.* Expense reimbursement should be limited to the actual cost of travel, food, and lodging reasonably incurred by a law clerk and, where appropriate to the occasion, by the law clerk's spouse. Any payment in excess of such an amount is compensation.

C. *Public Reports.* A law clerk should make and file such reports as may be prescribed by law or by the Judicial Conference of the United States.

Notwithstanding the above, a law clerk shall not receive any salary, or any supplementation of salary, as compensation for official services from any source other than the Government of the United States.

Canon 7

A Law Clerk Should Refrain from Political Activity

A. *Political Activity.* A law clerk should refrain from political activity; a law clerk should not act as a leader or hold office in a political organization; a law clerk should not make speeches for or publicly endorse a political organization or candidate; a law clerk should not solicit funds for or contribute to a political organization, candidate, or event; a law clerk should not become a candidate for political or public office; a law clerk should not otherwise engage in political activities.

Effective Date of Compliance

Persons to whom this Code becomes applicable should arrange their affairs as soon as reasonably possible to comply with it and should do so in any event within thirty days of the appointment.